Days of STEAM

Days of STEAM

TWO GENERATIONS OF RAILWAY PHOTOGRAPHY

NEIL DAVENPORT

Illustrated with photographs by the author and his father,
the late Arthur Davenport

Patrick Stephens Limited

First published in 1991

British Library Cataloguing in Publication Data
Davenport, Neil
  Days of steam: two generations of railway photography.
  1. English Photographs. Special subjects: Steam locomotives
  I. Title   II. Davenport, Arthur
  779.9385.361

ISBN 1-85260-335-6

Patrick Stephens Limited, a member of the Haynes Publishing Group plc, has published authoritative, quality books for enthusiasts for more than twenty years. During that time the company has established a reputation as one of the world's leading publishers of books on aviation, maritime, military, model-making, motor cycling, motoring, motor racing, railway and railway modelling subjects. Readers or authors with suggestions for books they would like to see published are invited to write to: The Editorial Director, Patrick Stephens Limited, Sparkford, Nr Yeovil, Somerset, BA22 7JJ.

Typeset by Burns & Smith Limited

Printed in Great Britain by J. H. Haynes & Co. Ltd.

Front endpaper *The Birkenhead-South Coast train, hauled by British Railways Standard class '4' 2-6-0 No 76056, passing through a cutting near Albury Common near Guildford on 23 April 1956.* *AD*

Opposite title page *'U1' Class 2-6-0 No 31899 passing Epsom Common Signal box on the 11.20 am through Epsom goods train to Norwood Junction, 25 August 1962. The signal box was closed in April 1964.*

Rear endpaper *A Worsdell 'J25' Class 0-6-0 recedes with a goods train for Penrith at 11.15 am on Thursday 5 July 1951. The train has just passed under the Settle-Carlisle line north of Appleby station.*

CONTENTS

ACKNOWLEDGEMENTS

I thank the following for their help in the realization of this book: the publishers for accepting with enthusiasm a personal story from an unknown author at a time when railway books are becoming ever more specialized; the Manager of the Tourist Information Centre at Appleby in Westmorland, for dates concerning the history of that beautiful town; the Information Assistant of the Regional Public Affairs Manager, British Railways Board, Southern Region, for dates which I failed to establish by observation of events in the Epsom area, and other important information; the Map Library of the British Library, for allowing me to see the large-scale maps which enabled me to include details of the track layout of the Horton Light Railway in my sketch-map; Miss Sheila Woodward, for providing the portrait of her grandfather Thomas Woodward; my mother, for allowing me to use two of her colour transparencies; and finally, my sister Jean for doing all the typing.

Those who read my preface will find that I have also not forgotten to thank those many railway authors whose books and articles have been so helpful to me.

PREFACE

My father was a railway enthusiast all his life and infected me with his love for the steam engine at what, if this book were on some other subject, I should describe without hesitation as a tender age. We both became keen railway photographers and took many hundreds of pictures. This book contains a selection of them which will, I hope, give a fair impression of what it was like to be a railway enthusiast in steam days.

Over three-quarters of the pictures were taken in the 12 years following nationalization on 1 January 1948, a period when the railways of Britain retained to a remarkable extent the character they had before the previous great amalgamation of 1923. To show how much the railway scene has changed since that period, I include a few comparison pictures taken more recently.

I chose the photographs in this collection to illustrate eight themes, each — bar the last — being a line or region which my father and I knew well. The themes relate to all four of the big prenationalization companies. To introduce each theme, I present the relevant history and describe some of the occasions on which the pictures were taken. I list the sources in which I found the historical, and much other, information at the end of this book, but thank the authors here for the help which their works have given me. The remaining facts come from notes which my father and I made at the time, and, of course, my memories.

INTRODUCTION

Thanks to the railway preservation movement, it is still possible to see and photograph, and often to hear and smell, a good variety of steam locomotives in Britain. But the present-day experience is very different from that of the time when thousands of steam engines were at work throughout the country. What I hope to do with this book is give an impression of what it was like to be a railway enthusiast then.

For our personal pleasure, my father and I took a great many railway photographs. Some were taken during journeys to and from work, but most resulted from our holidays and from special photographic expeditions. It is only fair to admit, as my mother and sister must have noticed, that we did not always make a very clear distinction between these last two categories of event. Obviously, a miscellaneous collection of our pictures would illustrate the great variety of the railway scene during the period in question, but I believe that I am more likely to achieve my aim by describing and illustrating in some detail a limited number of well-defined themes. My choice of themes is, of course, governed by my material and that, in turn, by the circumstances of my father's life and my own. That is why, before I can explain that choice, I must first present some family history.

My great grandfather, Henry Davenport, was manager of the Midland Railway wagon works at Bromsgrove, in Worcestershire. He was regarded with a mixture of awe and affection by the men, who nicknamed him 'Physic' — presumably to acknowledge their recognition of his being something rather unpleasant but good for them. Family tradition held that he was a patentee. When I started patents work in 1962 I soon found, from the 'Alphabetical Index to Inventors', that the story was factual. Patent No 16506 of 16 December 1886, 'Improvements in the Manufacture of Laminated Springs for Railway Carriages and Wagons and other Vehicles', was in the names of Henry Davenport of Station Villa, Bromsgrove, and Thomas Gething Clayton of 202, Osmaston Road, Derby, and described a frame in which a red-hot spring plate could be clamped during quenching to prevent its distortion. Clayton was the Midland's Carriage and Wagon Superintendent.

Henry Davenport and his wife, Anne Maria, had eight children. Arthur (1862–1944), the youngest of four who lived to a good age, was my grandfather. He started a railway career at his father's works, beginning each day at an astonishingly early hour — half past five, I believe. He went home for breakfast as well as for lunch! By the time he married, in 1891, he had transferred to the Midland Carriage and Wagon Works at Derby, and he lived in that town (a city only since 1977) for the rest of his life. He rose to be Chief Timber Inspector of the London, Midland and Scottish Railway, and I remember his showing me his beautiful leather-covered first-class pass for the whole of that system. I have the hammer with which he marked timber that he had approved.

Arthur Davenport married Alice, one of the daughters of another Midland Railway man, Thomas Woodward (1840–1925), who had been responsible for signalling when the Settle–Carlisle line was built in the early 1870s and by the time of his retirement had become Signal Engineer and Superintendent of the Midland Railway. Alice Woodward (1870–1948) was the second of five children borne by his second wife, Maria Mahala, and spent several years of her childhood at Appleby where her father lived during his Settle–Carlisle activities.

With his father, both grandfathers, and many other relations being railway men, it is not surprising that my father, Arthur Davenport (junior), became interested in railways when still a boy. What does surprise me is that he did not himself follow a railway career, but spent his working life with the National Provincial Bank. He started work for this Bank in January 1910 at the Lincoln Branch. In September 1913 he was moved to

Henry Davenport, my great grandfather.

Arthur Davenport, my grandfather.

Thomas Woodward.

My father, Arthur Davenport.

Burton-on-Trent and so could resume living at his home in Derby. He travelled to and from work by rail and, because of awkward train times, had to use different routes for his outward and homeward journeys. He went to Burton on the Great Northern from Derby (Friargate) and returned in a Midland or London & North Western train to the main, Midland, Derby station. There was a convenient evening train which stopped at Burton 'to set down only'. If one got into this one had to nip along the corridor and settle quickly to avoid being traced. A story of his from those days which I particularly like is of the notice appearing above some carriage windows which said 'PUSH TO CLOSE'. Wags had discovered that, with very little effort, this could be changed to read 'RUSH TO CLOSET'!

Arthur Davenport's business card and the hammer with which he indicated that timber had met with his approval.

From November 1915 until February 1919, my father served in the Royal Marine Artillery, first in Egypt and then in France and Belgium, on 15-inch howitzers. After demobilization he returned to the Bank in Burton-on-Trent but in September 1919 was moved to the City Office at 15, Bishopsgate in the City of London where he spent the remainder of his career. In 1934 he became Head of Country and Bill Departments (subsequently Bill Department), a post he held until he retired in 1953. When he first moved to London he lived in Beckenham, but upon his marriage he settled in Epsom where my sister Jean and I were born and still live.

Although a railway enthusiast from his boyhood and an amateur photographer throughout the period between the two World Wars, my father took only a few railway photographs during those years. The reason for this ghastly omission was that he satisfied his hunger for railway news and photographs with *The Railway Magazine* and commercial postcards. You will understand why his pre-war pictures have always seemed precious to me. I include four in this collection.

My father infected me with his own enthusiasm for railways at a very early age. I drew pictures of engines and trains, played with my clockwork 0 gauge Hornby railway and collected engine numbers on my holiday journeys. But my enthusiasm was LMS and LNER orientated, and I took no heed of the local Southern Railway steam activities. I have only slender recollections of the engines I saw during my walks along West Street, Epsom, to and from the Orchard School and later the prep school Kingswood House. In 1942 I went as a day-boy to Epsom College and it was a friend, Derek Lee, whom I met there, who opened my eyes to the interest of Southern locomotives. It was he, also, who introduced me to railway modelling. His father had built a fine model railway on trestles around what should have been the main front bedroom of his house, and I had the pleasure of helping to run this railway and contributing to its development: I made signals, both semaphore and colour light.

Derek's father, Frank Lee, was a pharmacist who inherited from his uncle, Mr Harsant, the fine chemists Harsant and Lee near Epsom Clock Tower. In those days the beautiful eighteenth-century shop had its original interior with wooden drawers part way up the walls behind the counters and handsome jars on shelves above, all bearing the Latin names of their contents. The old interior was removed by subsequent owners, Cross and Herbert, but the huge flasks of coloured water remain to enhance the beauty of the bow windows.

Over the next few years, my last at school, I went on many train-watching expeditions. These, together with holidays, enabled me to see some thousands of the locomotives then running, and to become familiar with almost all of their types. This latter process was helped by the appearance of the famous Ian Allan 'ABCs' which I bought in 1943.

In 1945 I left Epsom College and became a full-time chemistry student at the Royal College of Science in South Kensington. This is part of Imperial College, the other constituent colleges then being the City and Guilds College and the Royal School of Mines. In 1946, a group of railway enthusiasts formed the Imperial College Railway Society and I joined from the start. As well as talks by professional railwaymen and well-known amateur enthusiasts, the Society arranged visits, and the opportunities which these gave for photography were amongst the influences which led me to take up that excellent hobby.

Having obtained a BSc degree in 1948, I was enabled by my father's continuing kindness to carry out post-graduate research for just over two years. Towards the end of that time, in 1950, I started looking for a job

and went for interviews as far afield as Ruabon (Monsanto) and Manchester (ICI). Fortunately, it occurred to me that if I approached a photographic firm I might get a job which combined business with pleasure. The member of the college staff who helped students find work knew of several former students who had gone to Kodak Ltd, and suggested that I wrote to one of them. I did, and thus it came about that on the morning of 11 August 1950 I walked down the road from Harrow and Wealdstone station to the Kodak Works for an interview with the famous, kindly, but nevertheless somewhat awe-inspiring Dr Baines, Assistant Director of Research. I was offered a job, and on 1 January 1951 started what was to be a very interesting and pleasant period of 12 years working in the Research Laboratories. It was not until my second year with Kodak that I finished a thesis based on my post-graduate work and obtained a PhD degree. During my Harrow days I lived for most of the time near Belmont Circle, so the Stanmore Village branch was my local railway.

In 1962, the Kodak Ltd Patents and Trade Marks Department wanted another technical assistant. I was invited to accept this post and was allowed a six-month trial period in which I could find out about the work and then make up my mind whether or not to continue with it. I decided to do so and qualified as a patent agent in 1974. During my time with the Department it was housed in first one and then another High Holborn office, and I lived once more in Epsom. My daily train journey was to Waterloo and thus I saw the last days of main-line steam on British Railways. In 1985, Kodak Ltd decided to move the Patent Department to Harrow and since I could face neither a daily Epsom-Harrow journey nor a return to living in Harrow, I accepted an offer of early retirement.

Having presented this family history, I can more readily explain my choice of themes.

The first is Epsom, where I have lived for all except my Harrow years and where my father lived until his death in 1973.

The second is the Redhill-Reading line. This, the nearest all-steam line to Epsom, displayed a remarkable variety of engines in good scenery at the foot of the North Downs.

The third is London, through which all our holiday journeys passed and to which my father and I — and my sister also — travelled daily to work.

The fourth is Derbyshire, where both my parents were born and where my grandparents and other members of the family lived. Derby was a paradise for the railway enthusiast, and the beautiful Midland route to Manchester and that ancient and mysterious mineral line, the Cromford & High Peak Railway, were not far away. Derby was also on the Great Northern Railway Midland Extension from Nottingham.

The fifth is Appleby, where my father's mother spent several years of her childhood, and where my father, latterly with his own family, spent some delightful holidays. Appleby is on the beautiful, and recently reprieved Settle–Carlisle line, and in the times I illustrate had the additional attraction of being on the charming, ex-North Eastern Railway Eden Valley branch from Kirkby Stephen to Penrith.

The sixth is Whitby, and embraces both the spectacular Middlesbrough–Scarborough coastal route and the beautiful Whitby and Pickering railway — happily still in action. As a child before the war I was taken to Scarborough, sometimes when my father's parents were also holidaying there. After the war, my parents and I stayed at the more picturesque and interesting Whitby, and I have revisited the area several times since.

The seventh is Harrow, where I spent my early years with Kodak. Apart from offering the pleasures of the Euston main line and the Stanmore Village branch, Harrow was also served by the Metropolitan Line services from Baker Street through Chalfont and Latimer (for the Chesham branch) to Aylesbury, as well as the trains over the old Great Central main line from Marylebone to Sheffield and Manchester.

The eighth, and last, is the Imperial College Railway Society which I have already mentioned.

Readers who are railway photographers may like to know something of how my father and I took the pictures in this collection. Both my parents were amateur photographers from quite early in their lives, developing their own films by inspection in red safelighting, and contact printing the negatives they obtained either indoors on 'gaslight' paper or out of doors on 'printing-out-paper', usually 'Seltona'. As a child I much enjoyed watching these processes and absorbed the rudiments of them.

My father started his photography with one of the famous Vest Pocket Kodak cameras giving eight pictures of 2½ in × 1⅝ in on 127 size roll film. (Incidentally, the word 'vest' was American for a jacket, not English for an undergarment!) After changing briefly to the much larger (3¼ in × 4¼ in) quarter plate roll film format, he settled on the sensible, and deservedly popular, 2¼ in × 3¼ in size. His camera, giving eight such negatives on a 120 film, was a Butcher's Watch Pocket Carbine having a 9 cm focal length f4.5 Ross 'Xpres' lens in a 'Compur' shutter. He used this camera until the autumn of 1949 when he part-exchanged it for a new camera of the same format, an Ensign 'Selfix 8–20' with a 13 cm f3.8 Ross 'Xpres' lens in an 'Epsilon' shutter. This he used until early in 1956 when he bought an Ensign 'Selfix 16–20' camera giving 16 pictures 2¼ in × 1⅝ in per 120 size film. This camera also had the excellent 'Xpres' lens, this time of 75 mm focal length, in an 'Epsilon' shutter. He changed to the smaller format partly because of the 50 per cent economy in film and developing which it offered, and partly because my enlarger would, at that time, only accept the smaller negative size.

It was early in 1947 that I realized that what I should be doing was not merely observing the railway scene and noting what I saw, but photographing it. I therefore got out the family 'VPK' camera and after several visits to his shop managed to obtain a 127 size Kodak 'Super XX' film from Epsom's best-known professional photographer, Frank Woods. Until recently his name remained, in mosaic, in front of the door of what is now a health food shop in Waterloo Road. The first six negatives on that precious first film were spoilt by light leaking through pinholes in the camera's ancient bellows, but by some kindly dispensation of Providence, the last two, and most precious, were little harmed. They were of engines that used to work the railway which ran from transfer sidings at Ewell West to the mental hospitals just north of Epsom.

I was lucky indeed to get those pictures. From my first four films I only obtained a dozen reasonable negatives, the heavy casualties being due not only to the progressively enlarging bellows holes but also to my inexperience at dish development and the fact that the none too positive catch in the side of the camera, which one had to remove for loading and unloading a film, once allowed the side to drop right off!

After these disasters my father had the camera repaired by Kodak. In those happy, and now far off, days, spare parts were still available for old cameras, and the conscientious mechanic who did the work not only fitted a splendid new bellows but also refocused the lens, an f7.7 Kodak 'Anastigmat'. Consequently the camera gave much better definition, as almost 30 of the pictures in this book show.

A railway photographer whose highest shutter speed is one-fiftieth of a second is very restricted with regard to taking pictures of moving trains. In September 1948, therefore, I brought a second-hand Zeiss Ikon 'Ikonta' 520, dating from 1935 or '36, having an f3.5 'Novar' lens in a 'Compur-Rapid' shutter. Its performance was disappointing initially, but after the lens had been refocused the camera gave good results and I used it for 14 years, until 1962. Then I bought a camera which had earlier been beyond my means: a second-hand Zeiss-Ikon 'Super Ikonta 531'. This had the excellent f3.5 75 mm 'Tessar' lens in a 'Compur-Rapid' shutter and had the further advantages of being fitted with a coupled rangefinder and of having had the lens surfaces coated for a previous owner. It was the camera I used for black and white photography during the final years of British Railways steam.

In my last sentence I included the words 'black and white photography' advisedly, because from 1952 I took an ever-increasing proportion of my photographs as colour transparencies. My first 35 mm camera was a second-hand Kodak 'Retina', one of the early black ones with an f3.5 'Xenar' lens in 'Compur' shutter. After a year I decided that I should like to take all my pictures as 'Kodachrome' slides (as it turned out I never stopped taking black and white) and bought through Kodak Ltd a new 'Retina' IIa camera. This had an f2 Schneider-Kreuznach 'Xenon' lens in 'Synchro-Compur' shutter and just enabled me, in sunshine, to use 1/250th second exposure with the slow (ASA 10) 'Kodachrome' film of the day. I used this beautiful camera, marred only by a viewfinder which — by today's standards — was primitive, until 1969 when I succumbed to the temptation of buying a single-lens reflex camera, a 'Praktica' Super TL. That gave some good results but poor internal design rendered it liable to produce severe flare during long exposures. Although I was able to overcome this fault by making special lens hoods, I knew as soon as I read about the elegant, light-weight 'Olympus' OM-1 that that was the camera for me. I bought one as soon as possible, in April 1973.

Although I had used my 'Retina' IIa camera for a few negatives in the 'fifties and 'sixties, and my OM-1 for some in the early 'seventies, it was not until 1976 that I started to use 35 mm black and white film extensively. In April of that year I bought a 'Rollei' 35 camera which, as one of the smallest full-frame 35 mm cameras ever made, was suitable for carrying everywhere. Its 40 mm f3.5 'Tessar' lens gave results for an 8 in × 10 in print as satisfactory as those from the 'Super Ikonta', and this is the camera I have used for most of my black and white photography ever since.

I include the initials of my father (AD) at the end of the caption for each of his photographs, and acknowledge likewise the two colour transparencies taken by my mother with her initials (EDD).

1. EPSOM

Epsom, of Salts and Derby fame, is 15 miles south-west of London. It was not, after the pre-war electrification of the mid-Sussex route to Portsmouth, a place where a steam train enthusiast would have chosen to live. Yet the very scarcity of locomotive-hauled trains made those that one did manage to see particularly enjoyable.

Epsom has an interesting railway history, having been served, before the 1923 grouping, by two companies. It was first reached by the London, Brighton & South Coast Railway, which opened its station on Monday 10 May 1847. The line was, in effect, an extension of the old London & Croydon Railway, opened in June 1839, which in 1846 had amalgamated with the London & Brighton Railway to form the LB & SCR.

When the Epsom line was sanctioned by Parliament in 1844, it was intended that the whole London–Epsom route should be worked by the Clegg and Samuda atmospheric system (patent granted 3 January 1838, printed series No 7920). By this a train was, in effect, sucked along. A cast iron tube of 15-inch internal diameter and having a longitudinal slot at the top was laid between the rails. The slot was sealed with a valve made from metal and leather and lubricated with a mixture of beeswax and tallow. A special truck at the front of the train was attached to a piston in the tube by an iron connecting plate which traversed the slot. To propel the train, air was exhausted from the tube ahead of the piston by pumps in stations at intervals along the line. The haulage truck was provided with a mechanism for opening the valve ahead of the connecting plate and resealing it to the rear of that plate, ready for the next train. Atmospheric traction was introduced from Croydon to Dartmouth Arms in November 1845 and from there to New Cross in January 1847. Although the system shared many advantages with the later

Left 'U1' Class three-cylinder 2-6-0 No 31903 shunting at Epsom Goods on 17 December 1962.

electric traction, it was not altogether reliable and was unsuitable for complex track layouts. The LB & SCR stopped work on installing the system in December 1846 and abandoned its existing installations on 4 May 1847, a few days before the Epsom line was opened.

The next lines at Epsom were opened in 1859. On February a single-track, isolated line 3¾ miles long from Epsom through Ashtead to Leatherhead was brought into use, being worked by the London & South Western Railway. The line lost its isolation on 4 April when that company reached Epsom from Wimbledon. On 8 August the LB & SCR opened an extension from its original Epsom terminus to the end of the Epsom–Leatherhead line so that it too could run trains through to Leatherhead. The two companies had agreed, on 29 July, to own the line jointly and share use of the terminus at Leatherhead, just east of the Kingston Road. In November they set up a joint operating committee. These arrangements were subsequently approved by Parliament, the joint ownership by an Act of 23 July 1860 and the operating committee by an Act of 21 July 1863.

Somewhat surprisingly, the L&SWR and LB&SCR did not build a joint station at Epsom, but kept on using their own separate stations. The L&SWR station was on the site of the present Epsom station and had two platforms. That to the north, away from the town centre, was an island platform between two up lines carrying trains for Wimbledon and Waterloo. That to the south served a single down line but had a bay at the Ashtead end. LB&SCR trains used a pair of lines between those serving the L&SWR platforms and so could not stop at those platforms.

The joint line from Epsom did not terminate at Leatherhead for very long. On 4 March 1867 the old station was closed and two new stations were opened nearer the town. By then, also, the line from Epsom had been doubled. A week later the LB&SCR extended its route southwards to Dorking and soon afterwards, on 1 May, to Horsham.

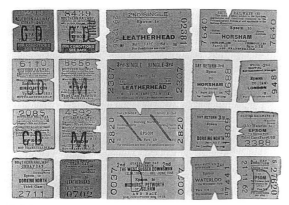

A selection of travel tickets.

A selection of local platform tickets.

Horsham was already quite an important railway centre standing on a line from Three Bridges — on the London to Brighton main line — down to the South Coast at Ford Junction on the Brighton to Portsmouth coastal route. Just to the south of Horsham there branched off a country route running north-west to Guildford and a second, more easterly, line down to the coast which joined the Brighton–Portsmouth route at Shoreham. Thus the opening of the Leatherhead–Horsham line placed Epsom on a pair of routes to the South Coast, one of which was the LB&SCR main line from London to Portsmouth.

The L&SWR did not extend its line beyond Leatherhead so soon. It was not until 2 February 1885 that it started using a line to Effingham Junction on a route also opened that day from Hampton Court Junction to Guildford. A station was opened at Effingham Junction on 2 July 1888.

The LB&SCR station at Epsom was by the Upper High Street, and much of the down platform station building remains, partly hidden by shops (see page 27). The roof was extensively repaired in the spring of 1978 following a fire. The two station platforms were staggered and a subway connected their rear ends. There was an engine shed by the up platform and a quite extensive goods yard. For a time after 1870 the station was named Epsom Town, to distinguish it from the L&SWR station, and the Southern Railway reinstated this name upon absorbing the two old companies in 1923.

When my father first lived at Epsom, his daily journeys to and from work were between Epsom Town and London Bridge, the trains usually hauled by Stroudley 'D1' 0-4-2 tank engines. On his first journey he was very surprised to encounter tunnels on the route, at Streatham and Tulse Hill, which were always full of noxious smoke. However, his steam suburban travel did not last long because the Waterloo to Dorking and Effingham services were electrified on 12 July 1925, and those from Victoria and London Bridge on 3 March 1929, when Epsom Town station was closed and a new station, on the site of the old L&SWR station, opened to handle all passenger traffic. The engine shed at Epsom Town was also closed, but the goods yard was kept for all heavier goods traffic, being renamed Epsom Goods. Some lighter traffic, including horse-box, parcels and mail trains, used loading bays at the new station. By the Transport Act of 1962 British Railways was freed of its legal obligation to act as a common carrier. Less than three years later, on 3 May 1965, Epsom Goods was closed. The site was cleared in 1974 and numerous houses were built upon it, the work starting in 1976.

The suburban electrification restricted steam haulage of trains through Epsom to the Bognor and Portsmouth services, occasional special trains and all goods and engineers' workings. The limited strength of some bridges prevented regular use of the heaviest Southern locomotives — such as those of the 'Lord Nelson', 'King Arthur' and 'Schools' Classes — so the coastal trains were hauled by the beautiful Brighton 'Atlantics' (classes 'H1' and 'H2'), 'Atlantic' tanks (class 'I3'), and 4-4-0s of all three pre-grouping companies. I can just remember being taken by my mother to Sutton for shopping before the war by steam train. My recollection is hazy in a literal sense — it is of getting into a corridor with steamed-up windows! The train was the 10.15 am and was the one up service which called at Epsom. The other coastal trains stopped at Dorking and Sutton only, I think mainly because they had longer platforms than those at Epsom. The era of main-line steam trains on the mid-Sussex route ended in July 1938, when the line from Dorking North to Havant was electrified, but certain features of the old timetable — including the 10.15 train to Sutton and Victoria — survived for many years.

An account of the railways at Epsom is not complete without a mention of the two branch lines which terminate at the eastern edge of Epsom Downs. The first was opened by the LB&SCR on 22 May 1865 and climbs from Sutton, on the Victoria–Epsom line, to a terminus called Epsom Downs. It was electrified on 17 June 1928. The terminus was designed to handle heavy race traffic and had nine platform faces, six of which were electrified. In 1972 all but one of the original platforms were put out of use and the faces of the platform retained, originally numbered 4 and 5, were renumbered 1 and 2.

For many years the particular glory of Epsom Downs station for the railway enthusiast was the magnificent array of LB&SCR wooden signals. They were eventually replaced by upper quadrant semaphore signals on new brackets, and these signals were used until 16 November 1981,

when the signal box was burnt down. A shuttle service to and from Sutton was instituted and ran until 4 October 1982 when colour light signals, controlled from the Victoria Signalling Centre (at Clapham Junction) were brought into use and allowed through services to London to be restored (see pages 44–45).

In 1987 or '88 the line at No 1 platform was removed, and the station closed altogether on Friday 10 February 1989. The following Monday a new station having a single platform came into use. The old station buildings were demolished at once to make way for the road of a housing estate being built on the site of the old station. The developers, Charles Church, constructed for the new station a delightful building, with walls of red brick and flint, well in keeping with the houses being built.

The other branch line to the edge of the Downs was that opened on Derby Day, 4 June 1901, by the SE&CR from Purley to Tattenham Corner. This terminus is nearer to the racecourse than Epsom Downs station, but has shrunk likewise, having only three of its original six platform faces in use. Some time between May 1985 and May 1987, when I looked in at the station during walks on the Downs, the fine signal box was taken down. The most interesting engines I saw at Tattenham Corner (on 24 July 1947) were two old SE&CR Class 'B1' 4-4-0s, Nos 1445 and 1454, disguised — not very convincingly — as Russian locomotives for use in making a film of *Anna Karenina*.

My enthusiastic observation of the Epsom railway scene started in 1943. I cycled past

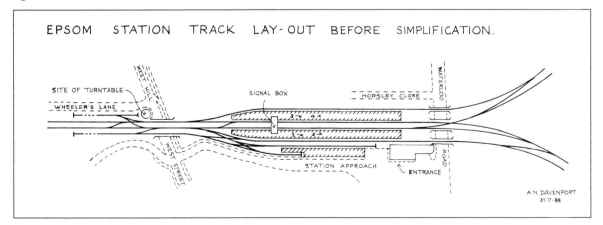

Epsom Goods on my way to and from school and got to know the ex-LB&SCR 0-6-2Ts which did the shunting and local goods train workings. Very occasionally there was one of Class 'E3', but usually the engine was an 'E4', or one of the four members of that class which had been rebuilt with a larger boiler as Class 'E4X' (see pages 22 and 24).

During the Second World War a number of Pullman cars were stored in the siding at Epsom Goods next to the up line, opposite Mill Road. They had lost their beautiful brown and cream livery which had been covered with matt paint, some cars grey and some a rusty brown. Unfortunately, I did not keep a separate note of the Pullman cars at Epsom but I did record named cars at Epsom Downs (October 1946) and Tolworth (Autumn 1943). The Epsom Downs cars, 'Cosmo Bonsor', 'Florence', 'Mimosa', 'Regina' and 'Valencia', were in a siding by the up line; those at Tolworth, 'Formosa', 'Maid of Kent', 'Milan' and 'Portia', were in a siding which still exists beside the down line. Throughout much of the year one may yet enjoy the sight of Pullman cars at Epsom when the stock of the Venice-Simplon-Orient Express wends its luxurious way to Arundel.

Immediately following the Allied invasion of Europe on D-Day, 6 June 1944, casualties were brought back to some of the LCC Epsom hospitals. Ambulance trains were run both to Epsom Downs and to Tattenham Corner, and Derek Lee and I saw some of these by extending our cycle journeys to and from Epsom College. The trains to Epsom Downs

Excerpt from page 16 of the 'Working Time Book of Freight Trains, commencing May 22nd 1944...', Southern Railway, London Central Division.

were double-headed because of the climb from Sutton, and we noted 'I3' No 2085 and 'C2X' No 2451 on 10 June (8.30 am), 'I3' No 2079 and 'C3' No 2301 on the 12th (6.00 pm), and two 'I3s', Nos 2077 and 2087, on the 14th. At Tattenham Corner, we saw 'N' Class No 1820 on 13 June and 'U1' Class No 1906 on the 15th.

The weekday freight workings at Epsom Goods were as follows, the times being taken from 1943 and 1949 Working Timetables. Some activities were very early in the morning and others were late at night, so to avoid confusion I quote the times using the 24-hour clock. At 0400 hrs a goods train left Norwood Junction for Epsom Goods, arriving at 0438 hrs. It left at 0500 hrs and after calling at Ashtead and Leatherhead, reached Dorking North at 0550 hrs. The engine ran light back

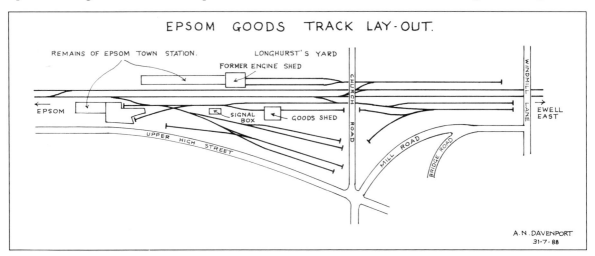

EPSOM GOODS TRACK LAY-OUT.

A.N.DAVENPORT
31-7-88

to Epsom Goods (the 1949 timetable gives a timing of 0723 to 0743 hrs for this) and then spent the morning there shunting. A second goods train left Norwood Junction at 0950 hrs and after pausing, for possible shunting, at Sutton, Cheam and Ewell East, arrived at Epsom Goods at 1236 hrs. Shortly afterwards (the 1949 timetable specifies 1245 hrs) the morning shunter left, running light to Sutton (see page 31). The second engine took the train which had been assembled during the morning to Norwood Junction, leaving at 1432 and arriving at 1507 hrs. In the evening an engine ran from Norwood Junction down to Dorking North. The 1944 timetable allows for the working of freight between Cheam, Epsom Goods and Leatherhead, the overall timing of the run being from 1739 to 2033 hrs. The 1949 timetable shows a light engine working from 1601 to 2005 hrs, the long journey time being due to stops at Epsom Goods and Ashtead. Finally, the engine took a train from Dorking North to Norwood Junction, leaving at 2230 hrs, passing Epsom at 2254 hrs and arriving at 2330 hrs (all 1944 times). If I was late getting to sleep, I could hear this train toiling up to the summit at Epsom Common.

The other local freight workings through Epsom were the legacy of the London & South Western Railway and ran between Guildford, Wimbledon and, ultimately, Nine Elms. These trains served the yards at Bookham, Leatherhead, Ashtead and Ewell West, and were usually worked by ex-L&SWR engines. I noted 4-4-0s of Classes 'D15', 'K10', 'L11' and 'L12', '700' Class 0-6-0s and, most interesting of all, 0-4-2 tender engines of the Adams 'A12' 'Jubilee' Class (No 614 on 20 September 1944 and No 620 on 7 August 1945). I include above the part of the 1944 time table showing these services; also a picture of the 3.44 pm (at Epsom) up train, my earliest shot of a moving target (see page 30).

The most impressive freight train through Epsom left Horsham at 10.28 in the morning, passed Epsom at 11.22 and reached Norwood Junction at 12.48. The train was often loaded to its maximum limit of 50 wagons and was usually hauled by a 2-6-0 or 2-8-0, although a Class 'Q' 0-6-0 sometimes appeared. During, and just after, the war, the 2-6-0's were ex-LB&SCR engines of Class 'K', and the first of

Excerpt from page 27 of the 'Working Time Book of Freight Trains, commencing May 22nd 1944...', Southern Railway, London Central Division.

these, No 2337, was painted in the full Southern Railway passenger livery of malachite green with black and yellow lettering and lining. The 2-8-0s were the Riddles design War Department engines Nos 7431/2/3/4 which were painted light khaki. Later on, Maunsell 2-6-0s of Classes 'N', 'U' and 'U1' were used, and also British Railways standard Class '4' 4-6-0s (see page 27). The last-named classes also took over the local freight workings, superseding the Class 'C2X' goods engines and larger radial-axle 0-6-2Ts of Classes 'E6' and 'E6X' (see pages 24–27) which had themselves gradually taken over from the 'E4s' and 'E4Xs'. The last traffic at Epsom Goods was handled by what are now called Class '33' diesel-electric locomotives (see page 28).

Besides the regular goods workings at Epsom there were occasional special workings for horse-boxes, parcels or mail which, as I have mentioned, used the bays at the passenger station. One saw these by chance or as a result of hearing a whistle from the engine and hurrying to the station. These small trains were often hauled by 'M7' 0-4-4Ts (page 97) or ex-LB&SCR 0-6-2Ts, but the Christmas mail specials were sometimes handled by more unusual engines such as Class 'B4X' and 'E' 4-4-0s.

Before leaving the topic of Epsom freight services, I must describe the most fascinating of them all, the carriage of coal from exchange sidings south of Ewell West station to the LCC Mental Hospitals, some 2½ miles to the east, by the Horton Light Railway. When the Long Grove Hospital was built, the contractors, Foster and Dicksee of Rugby, laid this railway to carry the building materials, and it was first used on 20 April 1905. The line originally crossed Hook Road, near West Ewell, by means of a level crossing, but in 1906 a woman was killed there so the track bed was lowered and a brick bridge built to carry the road over the line in its new cutting. This bridge survives (see page 34) and is the most substantial relic of the railway.

When, in 1907, Long Grove hospital had been completed, the LCC bought the railway for £9,300. A few years later, in 1911 and 1912, branches were laid, one to the Central Pumping Station and Electric Light Works, and the other to the site for a future hospital, West Park, which was built over the period 1915 to 1924.

The first engine of the Horton Light Railway was an 0-6-0 saddle tank named *Hollymoor*. This was replaced in 1935 by *Hendon*, another 0-6-0ST, built at Leeds by Manning Wardle and Co in 1926 Works No 2046. It had been used earlier by the contractors C.J. Wills and Sons Ltd when building the St Helier estate. I saw this engine, clean in its lined brown livery, more than once at Ewell West, but when I came to photograph it in April 1947 it stood, forlorn, in a siding near the engine shed at the Central Power Station, awaiting removal for scrapping (see page 32). A Robert Stephenson and Hawthorn 0-4-0ST, in a livery of medium green with black and white lining and red side-rods, had taken over its job. The new engine (also pictured on page 32) weighed 16¾ tons empty (21 tons in working order), had a boiler pressure of 160 pounds per square inch and carried 500 gallons of water. Stamped on the motion was the number, presumably the Works No, 7349.

The line was taken out of use in 1949 and the following year the track was lifted, starting from Ewell West, for sale. My last view of the engine was on 21 July 1951. Then the remaining track extended less than half a mile from the engine shed.

Early in July 1948 I was talking to shunting staff at Epsom Goods (see page 23) when one of them referred to the 'steamer' which came

through Epsom in the early morning. I was almost incredulous because I had tacitly assumed that all regular steam passenger workings had ceased in 1938 with the Portsmouth electrification. The timetable confirmed that there was each weekday a train from London Bridge (dep 0510 hrs) through Epsom (dep 0611 hrs) to Horsham (arr 0707 hrs), and that a train left Horsham at 0714 hrs which reached Brighton at 0824 hrs. It gave no hint that these two trains were one and the same. On 6 July I saw the train for the first time; it was hauled by 'U1' 2-6-0 No 1906. Naturally, my father and I decided that one day we would travel from Epsom to Brighton — 48 miles — by this unique steam service. The day proved to be 25 June 1949. We did our best to prepare for a memorable railway expedition by obtaining, in advance, permits for visiting Brighton and Eastbourne locomotive sheds. Our day was indeed outstanding owing to a succession of happy circumstances. The first was the weather — the sun shone throughout. The second was our discovery, when looking at — and, of course, photographing — the train at Horsham, that we could travel in the guard's compartment and enjoy a view ahead over the engine from the birdcage lookout (see page 40). The third was that most rare and desirable of privileges, an invitation to ride on the footplate (see page 41). Thus it came about that I travelled 8½ miles, from West Grinstead to Steyning, on 'N' Class 2-6-0 No S1825.

The remainder of our day was by no means an anti-climax. Eastbourne shed was almost entirely stocked with ex-LB&SCR engines, these being of Classes 'B4' and 'B4X', 'D1', 'D3', 'E5', 'E5X', 'I1X', 'I3' and 'K'. Perhaps the most interesting was 'B4' No 2068, pictured on page 41, which was still in pre-war livery, having elliptical cast numberplates on the cab and large numerals painted, under the word 'Southern', on the tender. The most interesting engines at Brighton shed were Marsh 'Atlantic' No 32037 *Selsey Bill* and a Stroudley 'D1' 0-4-2T, No 2253, in steam. Our journey back from Brighton to Horsham was, somewhat unsuitably, behind an ex-L&SWR engine, 'M7' 0-4-4T No 47.

Normally, those wishing to see the Brighton steam train had to get up very early. However, on 1 February 1963, a snowy day, I was waiting on Epsom station for my train to work when I saw a tell-tale line of steam rise in the distance. I had my camera with me so could photograph the train as it arrived behind British Railways Standard Class '4' 2-6-0 No 76055 at 8.0 am — nearly two hours late (see page 42).

My father and I travelled once again to Brighton on the 6.11 am train, on a more historic but less cheerful occasion: the day of the train's last run, 7 September 1963 (see page 42). The engine was British Railways Standard Class '4' 2-6-2T No 80094, and the train lacked a birdcage lookout!

All other steam passenger trains through Epsom were specials, some for Race Meetings, some for important foreign visitors, some arranged by railway societies and some excursions of diverse origin (see page 21). The earliest that I noted was at 3.35 pm on 6 March 1945. I had been into Epsom for a haircut and was sitting on the top deck of the 164 bus, which in those days started from the road along by the station, waiting to return to College where there came slowly through Platform 1 a train of 13 LMS carriages hauled by Class 'L' 4-4-0 No 1764 and 'E' Class 4-4-0 No 1514. Thus I had a grandstand view of the only double-headed train I ever saw at Epsom. The Stephenson Locomotive Society special of 3 May 1953 came nearest to recreating the pre-war scene, being hauled by Brighton 'Atlantic' No 32425 *Trevose Head* (see page 20). A ramblers' special, which my father and I joined at Epsom on 8 June 1958, was the 'West Sussex Downsman', which ran from Charing Cross via West Croydon to Midhurst and back behind 'Q' 0-6-0 No 30549.

The passenger and goods trains I have described were not the only workings which brought steam locomotives to Epsom. Occasionally one was lucky enough to see an engineers' train, a breakdown train or a light engine.

To give anything like a balanced account of the Epsom railway scene I must mention, and illustrate, the convenient, efficient and soulless electric trains in which my father, sister and I travelled to London and back so

many thousands of times. I confess that my earliest pictures of electric trains were due not to my enthusiasm for the subjects but to my attempts — happily successful — to improve the performance of my 'Ikonta' 520 camera. After refocusing the lens in April 1949 and again in October that year, I tested the camera by taking a few local pictures, including some of trains (see page 38).

Until some years after the Second World War, most of the Southern Electric suburban trains were of three, six or eight cars, consisting of one or two three-car units, or two such units with a pair of trailer cars sandwiched in between. The carriages had originally been pre-grouping steam train compartment stock. Each compartment had five-a-side seating and the window in each door could be lowered into a recess between the inner and outer door panels. A perforated leather strap was attached to the bottom of the window, and a brass pin to the top of the inner door panel. One could therefore lower the window and hold it at the desired level by putting the nearest hole in the strap over the pin. Unfortunately, the leather straps sometimes proved irresistible to vandals and when cut or removed only allowed the choice between and fug and a gale. The best plan was to sit with one's back to the direction of travel and hope that a braver passenger on the opposite seat would choose the gale.

In the late 'forties and early 'fifties, some of the three-car sets were extended to four cars by the addition of a steel-bodied six-a-side compartment coach. This was a temporary measure and the new trailer cars were later incorporated into 4-SUB units.

The corridor stock built for the 1938 Portsmouth electrification was heavily and comfortably built with fine wooden panelling inside (see page 38). It differed from the stock made for the Brighton main line by having corridor connections at the unit ends as well as between the cars within each unit. In 1949 a train of this stock was introduced, allegedly for the benefit of important railway officials living at Dorking, which called at Epsom (depart 9.14 am), Sutton and then Victoria. Thus it came about that I enjoyed a luxurious journey to town throughout my last two years at College.

Above *Class 'S11' 4-4-0 No 396 entering Epsom Station* 20 *on a Waterloo-Bognor excursion train, probably in the summer of 1932.* AD

Below *A Stephenson Locomotive Society special train, hauled by Class 'H2' 'Atlantic' No 32425* Trevose Head, *at Epsom Common summit on 3 May 1953.* AD

Above *A Derby Day special which left Epsom at 6.40 pm on Wednesday 30 May 1951 for its return journey to Hereford. The engine, class 'U' 2-6-0 No 31799, has just reached the top of the 1 in 100 climb to Epsom Common summit.* *AD*

Below *A Portsmouth-Victoria special train for the Soviet leaders Bulganin and Kruschev approaching the summit at Epsom Common from Ashtead. The Pullman cars are hauled by 'West Country' Class 'Pacific' No 34092 City of Wells. 18 April 1956.* *AD*

Above *A general view of Epsom Goods, 16 July 1949. The engine on the train of horse-boxes is 'E6' 0-6-2T No 32416. Note the former engine shed in what was then Longhurst's yard for building materials and timber.*

Below *'E4' Class 0-6-2T No 2476 at Epsom Goods at 12.15 pm on 28 December 1948. The round-topped windows are in the building which had been adjacent to the up platform of Epsom Town station.*

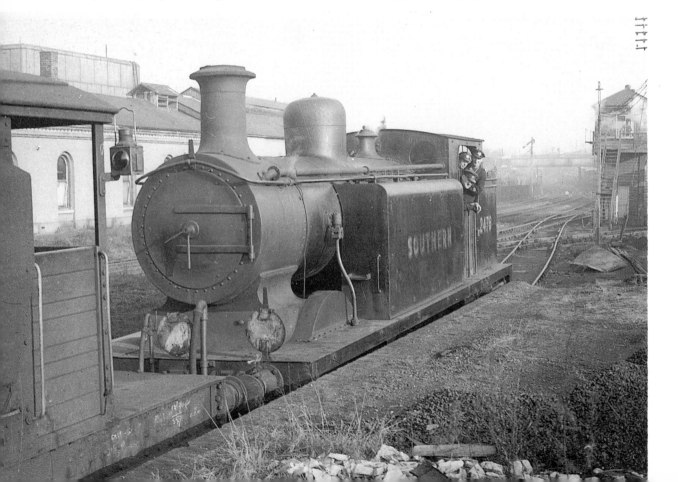

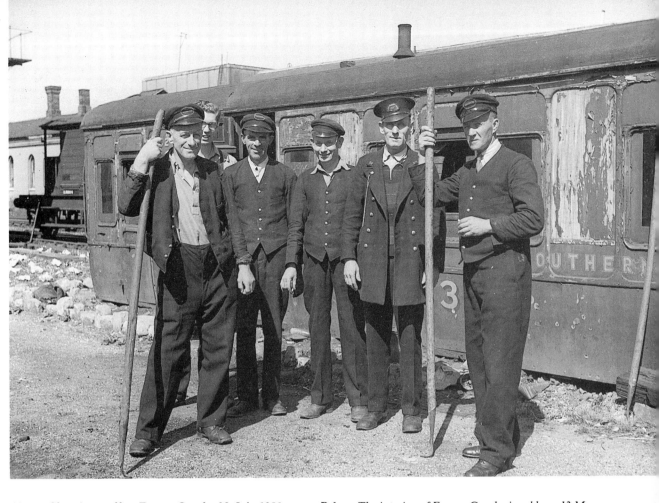

Above *Shunting staff at Epsom Goods, 28 July 1951.*   **Below** *The interior of Epsom Goods signal box, 13 May 1950.*   23

Above *'E6' Class 0-6-2T No 32416 at Epsom Goods bearing handsome, presumably hand-painted, lettering and numbering. 20 November 1948.*

Below *'E4X' Class 0-6-2T No 32466 at Epsom Goods on 30 December 1950. The engine is in full British Railways livery with lining and the lion-on-wheel emblem.*

Above *An 'E6X' Class 0-6-2T No 2411 at Epsom Goods on 10 November 1948. Church Road bridge, from which several pictures in this collection were taken, can be seen in the background. It was rebuilt in the summer of 1970.*

Below *The same engine after being fitted with a two-domed boiler. The water-tanks now bear the lion-on-wheel emblem. 2 June 1951.*

26 **Above** *'C2X' Class 0-6-0 goods engine No 32444 at Epsom Goods on 28 July 1950.*

Below *Class 'U' 2-6-0 No 31620 at Epsom Goods on a snowy Saturday morning, 19 January 1963.*

Above *British Railways Standard Class '4' 4-6-0 No 75074 shunting by Hall's yard, Epsom Goods, 23 September 1963.*

Below *Another Class '4' 4-6-0, No 75067, shunting at Epsom Goods on 25 September 1963. The engine is by the remains of Epsom Town station down platform. The old station building, now the only relic of that station, can be seen beyond.*

27

Above *Class '3' Bo-Bo diesel-electric locomotive No D6542 at Epsom Goods on 8 October 1963. This locomotive was later renumbered 33024 and designated as Class '33/0'.* AD

28

Below *A brake van bearing the legend 'To work between Epsom and Epsom Goods only'. The length of that journey was barely half a mile. 28 October 1950.*

Above *'Q1' 0-6-0 No 33035 passing Epsom Goods on a parcels special, 20 April 1963.*

Below *Over 25 years later, possibly the only carriages from steam days now running on BR, the Pullmans of the Venice-Simplon-Orient Express, pass the site of Epsom Goods on their way from Victoria to Arundel on Wednesday 6 September 1989. The locomotive was a Class '73' electro-diesel.*

Above *An 'E4' Class 0-6-2T approaching Mill Road bridge, Epsom, on 16 July 1949. This engine has been preserved on the Bluebell Railway as LB&SCR No 473 Birch Grove.*

Below *The 3.44 pm through Epsom goods train hauled by '700' Class goods engine No 701 on 13 May 1948. The timing of this train is shown on page 17. The train is about to pass under Castle Road bridge, which has recently — in the winter of 1987 — been repaired. The arch has been strengthened with reinforced concrete, the cement mixture for which was sprayed on, and the parapets have been rebuilt.*

Above *'E4' Class 0-6-2T No 32495 leaving Ewell East on the 1.10 pm train for Epsom Goods.*

Below *Class 'E6' 0-6-2T No 32416 running light through Ewell East station at midday on 21 January 1950.*

Above left Hendon, *the second engine to be used on the Horton Light Railway. It was built by Manning Wardle & Co Ltd of Leeds in 1926 and had the works number 2046. It had been used in the extending of the Underground to Hendon and Edgware and, later, by the contractors C.J. Wills and Sons Ltd during the building of the St Helier estate. The engine is here seen in the siding at the central power station awaiting removal for scrapping. 11 April 1947.*

Left *The new Robert Stephenson and Hawthorn 0-4-0ST which superseded* Hendon, *photographed at Ewell West on 10 November 1947. The number stamped on the motion, and so presumably the works number, was 7349. Weights were: empty 16¾ tons; working order, 21 tons. Working pressure was 160 psi and water capacity was 500 gallons.*

Above *A Horton Light Railway train at the level crossing with the footpath which runs from Hook Road past St Ebba's Hospital to Chessington Road, Ewell West. Note the shadow of the footbridge from which this picture was taken on 31 December 1948.*

Above right *A Horton Light Railway train coming under the footbridge which carried the footpath from Horton Lane to Chessington, 29 December 1948.*

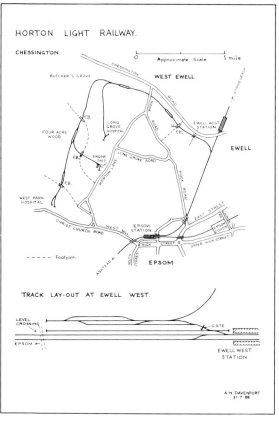

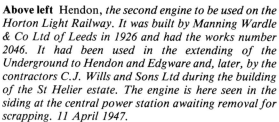

Above *The 0-4-0ST outside its shed at the central power station, 14 July 1948.*

Left *The bridge which carried Hook Road over the Horton Light Railway near West Ewell photographed on 21 January 1950. The bridge still exists.*

Above right *Taking up the track of the Horton Light Railway on 22 April 1950. The demolition train is near where Longmead Road now approaches Chessington Road, West Ewell. St Ebba's Hospital is in the background.*

Right *The central span of the footbridge at the level crossing shown in the picture on page 33 falling after being cut with an oxy-acetylene torch. 1 April 1950.*

Above *Epsom station entrance on 1 October 1950. Apart from some damage to the painted glass signs, the entrance had not altered since opening in 1929.*

Below *The elegant new lettering provided by British Railways, photographed on 16 December 1962. The author was sorry to see this fine lettering replaced by the substitutes shown in the next two pictures.*

Above *The British Rail fascia at Epsom, photographed on 24 June 1987, not many months before the Network SouthEast fascia was provided.*

Below *The Network SouthEast fascia photographed on 24 October 1987, very soon after it had been fitted. A new station entrance incorporated in an office building is due to be built within the next year or two.*

Above *A London Bridge to Dorking North train leaving Epsom on 2 October 1949. The train, unit S4533, is a four-car unit made up by including in an early three-car unit a trailer car built for subsequent use in a Class '405/2' unit.*

Below *A down coastal train passing Epsom Goods on 4 August 1962. The train is made up of the four-car corridor sets introduced just before the Second World War for the Portsmouth services.*

Above *The signal gantry at Epsom just before its replacement by the colour light signals shown below. 23 February 1966.*

Below *The colour light signals shown in the picture above before their replacement by the new signals*

bearing cancellation crosses, 20 June 1987. The new signals were brought into use on 11 October 1987 and came under the control of the Waterloo signalling centre (at Wimbledon) when Epsom signal box was closed at the end of July 1990.

Above *A 'U1' class 2-6-0 on the 6.11 to Brighton nearing Castle Road bridge, Epsom Common, on 1 July 1950.*

40

Below *The 6.11 from Epsom to Brighton in Leatherhead station on 25 June 1949, the day when my father and I made our first journey on the train. The engine was 'N' Class 2-6-0 No S1825. We travelled much of the way in the guard's van shown.*

Above *The author enjoying his longest footplate ride, between West Grinstead and Steyning. My father took this picture from the 'birdcage' lookout shown in the previous picture.* *AD*

Below *'B4' Class 4-4-0 No 2068 in its pre-war livery at Eastbourne shed, 25 June 1949.*

Above *Delayed, presumably by the snow, the 6.11 am to Brighton leaves Epsom at 8.0 am hauled by British Railways Standard Class '4' 2-6-0 No 76055. 1 February 1963.*

Below *My father and I travelled to Brighton on the last London Bridge-Epsom-Brighton steam train, which ran on 7 September 1963. The engine, a British Railways Standard Class '4' 2-6-4T, is here shown at Dorking North. The bridge in the background carries the Redhill-Reading line.*

Above *British Railways Standard Class '5' 4-6-0 No 73114 at West Street bridge, Epsom, with a breakdown train on 4 March 1966.* *AD*

Below *'The Surrey Downsman Rail Tour' of the Locomotive Club of Great Britain approaching Epsom station on 5 March 1967. The locomotive, No 34087 (formerly 145 Squadron) was the last steam engine I saw at Epsom. Steam traction on the Southern Region ceased in July 1967.*

Above *Former LB&SCR wooden signals at Epsom Downs, 11 June 1950.*

Below *The upper quadrant signals which replaced the old signals shown above, photographed on 2 March 1963.*

Above *The colour light signals controlled from the large box at Clapham Junction which replaced the signals shown in the previous picture. The old signal bracket was removed soon after this picture was taken on 15 September 1983.*

Below *My only photograph of a steam locomotive at Epsom Downs: rebuilt Bulleid 'Battle of Britain' Class 4-6-2 No 34089 602 Squadron in platform 2 on Sunday 5 June 1966 at the head of 'The Surrey Rambler' rail tour.*

Above *Ashtead station before rebuilding, November*   **Below** *Ashstead station after rebuilding, 24 April 1987.*
1966. Rebuilding started in March 1968.

Above *'M7' Class 0-4-4T No 22 leaves Leatherhead on a goods train for the Effingham Junction and Guildford line on 28 December 1948.*

Below *Marsh 0-6-0 goods engine No 2307 of Class 'C3' (built at Brighton in 1906) at the goods yard adjoining Dorking North station on the morning of 24 August 1948.*

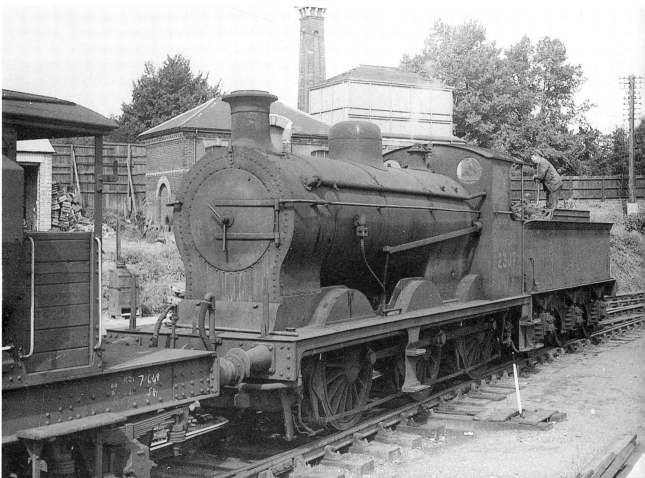

2. REDHILL TO READING

Of railways near to Epsom, the one which my father and I most liked to visit was the 20-mile stretch from Redhill to Guildford of the Redhill-Reading line. This runs at the foot of the North Downs through what, for the Home Counties, is notably fine scenery. Only the first mile and three-quarters at the eastern end, from Redhill to Reigate, has been electrified, and until the early 'sixties all trains west of Reigate were steam-hauled. Diesel multiple units took over the stopping passenger services at the beginning of 1965, and the use of steam locomotives on freight trains ceased at the end of that year.

The Redhill-Reading line was opened in stages in 1849. A section of the route, from Shalford — just south of Guildford — to Ash — about five miles further towards Reading — was owned by the L&SWR, from whom running powers were obtained. The remainder was bought in 1852 by the South Eastern Railway.

The line almost certainly owes its survival not to its local traffic but to its usefulness as a link between the south-east corner of England and the many places to the north and west which are accessible from Reading. From 1897 until 1964 there was a South Coast to Birkenhead through service which, with its brown and cream Great Western stock, was the most handsome train I saw on the line. It was usually hauled by a Maunsell 2-6-0, perhaps surprisingly in view of the fact that engines of Great Western origin quite often worked to Redhill and back (see page 61). When job hunting during my last year at College, I travelled to Ruabon on the Birkenhead service for an interview with Monsanto Chemicals.

One of the attractions of the Redhill-Reading line was the great variety of locomotive classes which worked along it.

Between us, my father and I saw 35 classes, namely:

ex-LB&SCR	'B4X' (4-4-0), 'C2X' (0-6-0), 'K' (2-6-0)
ex-L&SWR	'L11', 'L12' (4-4-0s), 'M7' (0-4-4T), 'S11', 'T9' (4-4-0s), '700' (0-6-0)
ex-SE&CR	'B1' (4-4-0), 'C' (0-6-0), 'D', 'E', 'E1', 'F1' (4-4-0s), 'H' (0-4-4T),'L', 'L1' (4-4-0s), 'N' (2-6-0), 'O1' (0-6-0)
ex-SR	'BB' (4-6-2), 'Q', 'Q1' (0-6-0s), 'S15' (4-6-0), 'U', 'U1' (2-6-0s), 'V' (4-4-0)
ex-WD	'Austerity' (2-8-0)
ex-GWR	'4300' (2-6-0), '6100' (2-6-2T), '7800' (4-6-0)
ex-LMS	'4' (Fairburn 2-6-4T)
BR	Standard '4' (4-6-0), '4' (2-6-0), '4' (2-6-4T)

Many occasional visitors must have eluded us.

There were three locomotive sheds on the Redhill-Reading line, at Redhill, Guildford and Reading. I visited the first two of these on several occasions, sometimes with an official permit and sometimes with impromptu permission given by a sympathetic shed foreman. Even when circumstances prevented a visit, one could see much of the activity at both sheds, from a hill at Redhill (see page 52) and from a road bridge at Guildford.

A selection of Redhill-Reading line tickets.

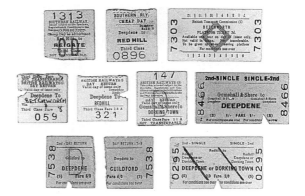

Left *A Guildford train near Shere. 'N' Class 2-6-0 No 31864 pilots another engine of that class on a three-coach train, presumably to save the trouble of a light engine working, on 23 April 1956.*   *AD*

The station on the Redhill-Reading line nearest to my home at Epsom is Betchworth, halfway between Reigate and Deepdene (Dorking). Quite often I cycled there, the climb up to Headley being rewarded by a dizzy descent of Pebble Coombe. Betchworth station is good for train photography and used to be better still, having a goods yard and, on the north side, a connection with a private railway system serving the quarry of the Dorking Greystone Lime Company. This system had portions of three different gauges, 3 ft 2¼ in gauges lines being used to bring stone from the quarries to the lime kilns, 18 in gauge lines being used to serve drying sheds, and standard (ie 4 ft 8½ in) gauge lines being used to take the product from the works down to the connection near the station. The 3 ft 2¼ in and standard gauge lines were worked by steam locomotives, the narrow gauge engines being 0-4-0Ts named *Townsend Hook*

(see page 58) and *William Finley*. The standard gauge engines were also 0-4-0Ts, one being named either *Baxter* or *Captain Baxter* (for the cause of this doubt, see my father's photograph of the water tank on page 57), and the other being a vertical-boiler engine nicknamed the 'coffee-pot' (page 58). In December 1949 I obtained permission at the office to look round the works and took pictures showing the kilns (see page 59). Had I known, as I do now, how extensive the workings were, I should have explored further.

After retiring from work my father had plenty of time in which to discover viewpoints for photography. For a number of years he enjoyed the advantage of a permit for trackside photography on non-electrified routes, and built up a collection of pictures of which it is hard to give a just impression with only a few examples.

Wainwright ex-SE&CR Class 'E' 4-4-0 entering Reigate station on a Redhill train at 4.45 pm on 25 September 1948.

Above *Drummond 'T9' Class 4-4-0 No 30732 on an up train in Reigate station, 4 April 1959.* *AD*

Below *British Railways Class '4' 2-6-4T No 80144 on a short train in Reigate station, 18 January 1964.*

51

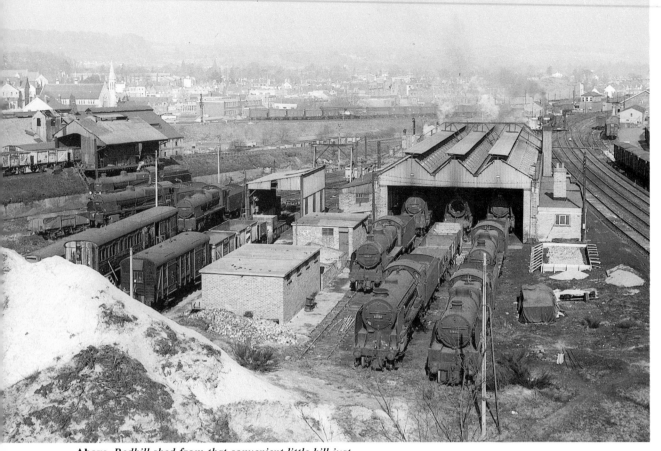

Above *Redhill shed from that convenient little hill just to the south, 2 March 1963. The large-chimneyed 'Schools' Class 4-4-0 in the foreground is No 30930 Radley.*

Below *Former GWR '4300' Class 2-6-0 No 6363 at Redhill shed on 30 December 1949.*

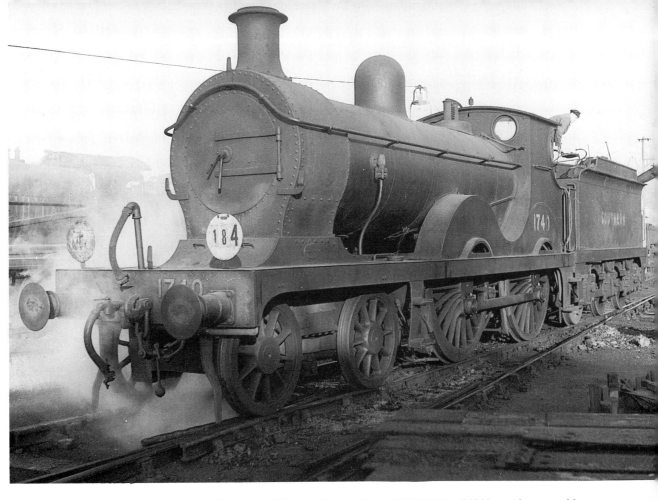

Above *Wainwright Class 'D' 4-4-0 No 1740 at Redhill shed on 30 December 1949.*

Below *Class 'U' 2-6-0 No 31800 on the turntable at Redhill shed, 14 September 1963.*

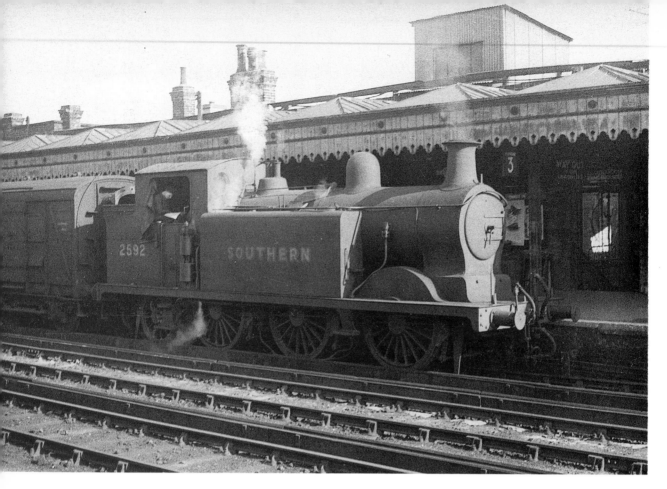

Above *Class 'E5' 0-6-2T No 2592 at Redhill station at*
12.20 pm on 29 February 1948.

Below *A period piece: Class 'H' 0-4-4T No 31550*
stands in Redhill station on the 3.06 pm train for
Tonbridge made up of former SE&CR stock, including
birdcage lookouts. 14 April 1951.

54

Above *'4300' Class 2-6-0 No 6394 on a relief express to Birkenhead approaching the level crossing at Betchworth station, 3 April 1956.* AD

Below *Maunsell Class 'N' 2-6-0 No 31851 leaving Betchworth at 1.34 pm on 29 February 1948 on a Redhill train. Notice the lorry loaded with milk churns waiting at the level crossing and also the office of the Dorking Greystone Lime Co, scenes at whose works are included later.*

55

56

Left *'N' Class 2-6-0 No 1406 on the 11.45 am train to Reading standing in Betchworth station, 29 February 1948.*

Below left *The first of Bulleid's ugly, but powerful, 'Q1' Class 0-6-0s, No C1, entering Betchworth with a pick-up goods train on 19 February 1949. This engine, later renumbered 33001, is part of the National Collection and is currently kept on the Bluebell Railway.*

Right *Dorking Greystone Lime Co standard gauge 0-4-0T Baxter at Betchworth, 3 April 1956.* AD

Below *Baxter's name, number and builder's plates. Should one take heed of the more polite painted name Captain Baxter? The engine is presently on the Bluebell Railway, beautifully restored in a handsome red livery as* Baxter. AD

Above *Dorking Greystone Lime Co vertical boiler 'coffee pot' geared locomotive built by T.H. Head of Middlesbrough at Betchworth, 22 December 1949.*

58

Below *No 4 Townsend Hook at Betchworth. This engine was Fletcher Jennings No 1721, built in 1880, and was photographed on 8 July 1948. It is preserved at the Chalk Pits Museum, Amberley.*

Above *The line of kilns at the Dorking Greystone Lime Co's works on 22 December 1949.*

Below *Small tip wagons on a standard gauge wagon at Betchworth on 22 December 1949.*

Above *A fine array of signs at the level crossing giving access to Brockham Warren, two miles east of Dorking on the Redhill-Reading line. 3 September 1949.*

Below *Former GWR '6100' Class 2-6-2T No 6130 entering Deepdene station, Dorking, on the 11.20 am train to Reading, 18 November 1950.*

Above *Class 'U' 2-6-0 No 31802 on the Birkenhead express nearing Dorking Town, with Box Hill in the background. The train had left Redhill at 11.40 am. 18 February 1950.*

Below *'B1' Class 4-4-0 No 1457 on a Redhill train below Box Hill in 1949.*

AD

61

Above *British Railways Standard Class '4' 2-6-0 No 76031 arriving at Dorking Town station on a down train, 23 November 1963.*

Below *Class 'S15' 4-6-0 No 30837 on an eastbound freight train near Shere, 29 April 1959.*   *AD*

Above *A Guildford train approaching Dorking, 7 September 1956. Two 'birdcage' sets are hauled by Class 'D' 4-4-0 No 31574, one of those built in 1907 with four cab windows.* *AD*

Below *An eastbound goods near Shere, hauled by Maunsell Class 'Q' 0-6-0 No 30533, on 16 July 1956.* *AD*

63

Above *Hawthorn Leslie 0-4-0ST* Ironside, *Works No 2175, built in 1890 for the Southampton Dock Co. As Southern No 3458 and BR No 30458, it was used for many years at Guildford shed for moving 'dead' locomotives and is seen here on 7 April 1950.*

Below *'USA' Class 0-6-0T No 30072, built by Vulcan Ironworks for the US Army Transporation Corps and bought by the Southern Railway in 1946, who modified the cab and coal bunker. This engine took over the duties of* Ironside *as shed pilot at Guildford. Note the new shed roof. 24 March 1963.*

Above *'0395' Class 0-6-0 goods engine No 30574 of Adams LSWR design built in the 1880s, and seen at the coaling plant by Guildford station on 17 September 1955.*

Below *Class 'T14' 'Paddlebox' 4-6-0 No 459 at Guildford coaling plant on the evening of 28 August 1948.*

65

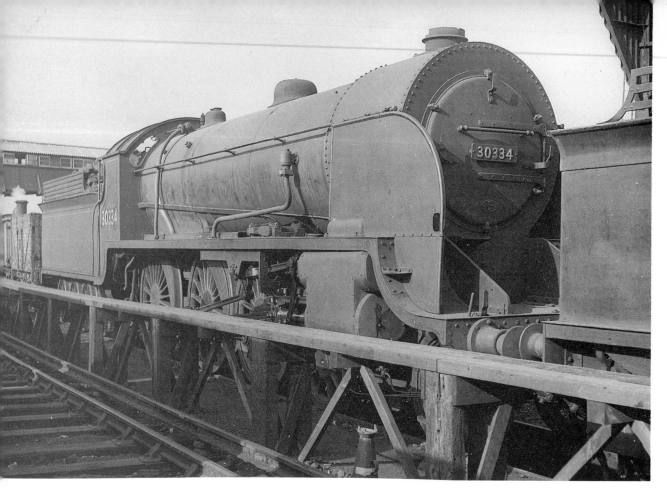

Above 'H15' Class 4-6-0 No 30334 near the coaling stage at Guildford on 17 September 1955. This engine was a 1924-25 Urie rebuild of the 1905 Drummond Class 'F13' 4-6-0.

Below Ex-LMS Class '5' 4-6-0 No 45346 on the 3.53 pm train to Reading standing in Guildford station on 21 September 1964.

AD

66

Above *A change of engines for the Wolverhampton express at Reading General on the day (15 June 1950) when I travelled on that train from Guildford to Ruabon. The engine to be replaced was 'U1' Class three-cylinder 2-6-0 No 31895...*

...and **below** *the replacement engine, No 4076* Carmarthen Castle.

3. LONDON

Until his retirement in 1953, my father commuted between Epsom and London for some 30 years. He probably never realized that this was what he was doing because the American usage of the verb 'commute', meaning 'to hold a season ticket and travel daily by train between a suburb of a city and that city', was not adopted here until, I guess, the 'sixties. My own preponderant railway experience of London was also as a commuter, first from 1945 to 1950 as a student and then from 1962 to 1985 as an office worker.

Our journeys to London were not all for business, however. Apart from those at the start of holidays, and those needed for visits to museums, theatres, exhibitions, concerts and, of course, shops, there were many made solely for the pleasure of watching and photographing trains. What we enjoyed most was to spend an hour or two at each of a number of termini, something which — thanks to the Inner Circle (now called the 'Circle Line') — was readily done.

Anyone wanting a detailed account of London's termini must read Alan Jackson's fine book. My aim is to present pictures and jottings which conjure up something of the atmosphere of the principal termini, and of Clapham Junction and Kensington Olympia.

Euston

Although not the oldest terminus — London Bridge opened one year earlier, in 1836 — Euston always seemed to be the most important. It was here that we saw the finest locomotives of our favourite railway, the London, Midland and Scottish. Architecturally it was a jumble, comprising an imposing arrival side (Platforms 1 to 6) to the east, a largely suburban middle (Platforms 7 to 11), and a rather unimpressive series of departure platforms (12 to 15) to the west (see page 74).

Left *The much lamented Euston arch, 24 August 1953.*
AD

The buildings included the famous Euston arch seen opposite, a splendid portico, whose destruction was a calculated and unnecessary act of vandalism. They also included a magnificent Great Hall which, one has to admit, was a more justifiable victim of the reconstruction, between 1962 and 1968, of the whole station (see page 75).

For a railway enthusiast, the platform with faces 2 and 3 was the Mecca, its curving roof on slender iron columns providing a perfect setting for Stanier's handsome 'Pacifics', as in the photograph on page 74. The far end gave views of all workings in and out of the station.

When I first visited Euston, London & North Western engines were still to be seen. For example, on 13 January 1944, Derek Lee and I saw Webb 0-6-2Ts 27666 and 27674, and one of the famous 'Cauliflower' 0-6-0s, No 28531, but by the time I had taken up photography, empty stock and other miscellaneous workings had been taken over by more modern locomotives.

St Pancras

A few minutes walk to the east from Euston, along a stretch of the Euston Road then filled with scruffy shops and used-car dealers, but now boasting a fire station, a library and a theatre — and soon to boast the new British Library building — brought one to St Pancras. As the starting point for holidays and visits to grandparents, this was my favourite terminus. With its splendid single-arched roof, 100 feet high and of 245 feet

Platform tickets from some London termini.

span, and its ornate Victorian gothic architecture, it is arguably the most individual and striking of all London's termini. It opened in 1868 and allowed the Midland Railway trains to run into London over their own metals, instead of relying on the grudging hospitality of the Great Northern Railway and running over the lines of that company from Hitchin to King's Cross.

The natural viewpoint at St Pancras is the end of Platforms 5 and 6. From here one used to see 'Jubilee' and Class '5' 4-6-0s on the principal trains (see page 77), 'Compounds' and various types of 2-6-2T and 2-6-4T on the suburban services and, perhaps, a smaller Midland tank acting as station pilot.

How pleasant it was, at the end of a journey when night had fallen, to walk past the cab of the engine and see the crew, illuminated by a flickering golden light from the open firebox door, contentedly leaning from their cab. A few steps more and one felt the glow from the hot boiler and heard that subdued simmering so characteristic of an engine in steam. The feelings engendered by this romantic end to a steam train journey were rapidly dismissed as one went, by tube or taxi, to Waterloo and ground one's way back to a chilly home by Southern Electric.

King's Cross

King's Cross lies a few steps to the east of St Pancras and was opened by the Great Northern Railway on 14 October 1852. It too has a natural viewpoint, the far end of departure platform No 1 (page 18). From here one sees the mouths of the tunnels which restrict entry to the station and which used to direct the lovely, mellow sound of a Gresley chime whistle towards the waiting enthusiast. From here, also, one saw a small locomotive coaling plant and the smoky efforts of suburban trains to climb out of the tunnel leading from the Underground lines.

The main aim of a visit to King's Cross was to see the 'Pacifics', streamlined and other, which handled so many of the principal trains. However, in my earlier train-watching days, the Great Northern 'Atlantics' were still in evidence. The suburban trains were formed of articulated sets of carriages hauled by Great Northern 0-6-2Ts of classes 'N1' and 'N2', as pictured on page 78.

Liverpool Street

Liverpool Street was one of the last of the London termini to open, doing so by stages in 1874 and 1875. The Great Eastern Railway had previously used a terminus at Shoreditch dating from 1840.

For the steam enthusiast, Liverpool Street was remarkable. What it lacked in the way of large locomotives — until the days of the 'Britannia' Class (page 81) there were no 'Pacifics' — it made up for by the sheer abundance of its traffic. For example, on 17 December 1943 my father and I noted seven 'Sandringham' ('B17') Class and 17 'B12' Class 4-6-0s, and the third of the new Thompson 'B1' 4-6-0s, No 8302 *Eland*. On other long-distance services were five rebuilt 'Claud Hamilton' 4-4-0s, including the engine, No 7770, bearing that name, and six Gresley 2-6-2s of Classes 'V1' and 'V3'. On suburban trains were shoals of Great Eastern suburban tank engines, including eight 2-4-2Ts of Classes 'F4', 'F5' and 'F6' and no fewer than 37 'N7' 0-6-2Ts. A grand total of 88 locomotives, seen in two hours or so, was made up with a 'J68' and a 'J69' 0-6-0T, and a 'J15' 0-6-0 goods engine. All these engines were fitted with the Westinghouse brake, and the panting noise of the steam-worked air compressors is one of my most powerful memories of that bustling era.

The place which gave a fine view of all the activity was the cab approach, a ramp rising from between Platforms 10 and 11 to a bridge across the lines into the station (see page 80). It was beside the small locomotive yard, and I spent many a happy hour there, arriving home with white circles around my eyes as evidence of the engine smoke in which I had been contentedly immersed.

Liverpool Street is close to Bishopsgate, where my father worked, and I would sometimes call in to see him and have the pleasure of being taken to the Great Eastern Hotel for a fine lunch. The station was a magnet for him, as well as for me, and it was he who took the pictures which best illustrate that smoky paradise.

Marylebone

A strong contender for the title of 'London's most peaceful terminus' is Marylebone. It was the last to be opened, in 1899, and the first to be shorn, in 1966, of its long-distance services: those to Leicester, Nottingham, Sheffield and Manchester along the old Great Central main line.

Until after the Second World War, the engines at Marylebone were predominantly of Great Central origin, with 4-6-0s, 'Atlantics' and 'Director' Class 4-4-0s handling the main line trains, and Class 'A5' 4-6-2Ts (page 82) the outer suburban services to Aylesbury and High Wycombe. The Great Central tender engines were soon supplanted by LNER locomotives, notably 'A3' 'Pacifics' and 'Sandringham' Class 4-6-0s. The 'A5' tanks lasted longer but were gradually replaced by 2-6-4Ts of LNER (class 'L1') and LMS design.

Paddington

When the Great Western Railway first reached London from Bristol, in 1841, their line ended at a temporary station at Paddington, which was then at the western edge of London. It was not until 1854 that the company was able to open a proper terminus, built a little to the east of the old station. What we know today is the result of several major reconstructions of the 1854 terminus.

In steam days Paddington was a world apart; the green-liveried 'Kings', 'Castles', 'Stars', 'Halls' and other 4-6-0s, with their copper-capped chimneys and wealth of polished brass, were splendidly different from anything to be seen elsewhere in London, even if they were, to my mind, disappointingly similar amongst themselves. The strong family resemblance of the various classes was due to the fact that at the 1923 grouping, the Great Western absorbed only minor railways and so was able to maintain unbroken the design tradition at its Swindon Works.

As with the other termini I have so far mentioned, Paddington has a viewpoint which eclipses all others, the end of Platforms 8 and 9 (see page 85).

London Bridge

London Bridge was the first railway terminus in London, being opened in 1836 by the London & Greenwich Railway. It grew to be a station with two distinct portions, the southern being a terminus for the LB&SCR and the northern a part-terminus, part-through station of the SE&CR. The through portion was on lines opened in 1864 to new termini on the north bank of the Thames at Cannon Street and Charing Cross.

The Brighton side of the terminus was badly damaged during the Second World War and was repaired only recently. The steam-hauled traffic there was handled by various ex-LB&SCR classes of engine including the Marsh 'Atlantics', (L240) Class 'IlX' and 'I3' 4-4-2Ts, and latterly by Fairburn (see page 86) and British Railways Standard Class '4' 2-6-4Ts. The South Eastern side handled traffic into Kent, including the coastal towns, which was hauled by various classes of ex-SE&CR 4-4-0s, 'King Arthur' and 'Schools' Class engines and, more recently, Bulleid 'Pacifics' (see page 87).

Victoria

Like London Bridge, Victoria became a terminus with two distinct parts. The first to open, in October 1860, was that to the west, built for the LB&SCR. The eastern side, built for the London Chatham & Dover and Great Western Railways, opened almost two years later in August 1862. The services provided by the Great Western were to last from 1863 to 1915.

The most memorable feature of Victoria was the great length of the Brighton platforms, each of which could hold two trains end to end. A third line was provided between each pair of lines serving the outer platform portions to give independent access to the inner portions. When, on my way to College, I went to a platform end to watch or to photograph trains, I certainly obtained good exercise.

The locomotives to be seen in the Continental and Brighton sides of the terminus were much as I have described for the equivalent sections of London Bridge.

Maunsell 2-6-0s were fairly common in Victoria and for a time the fine 4-6-2Ts surviving from the LB&SCR, Nos 2325 and 2326 (page 90), were to be seen. The Brighton 'Atlantics' were sometimes used on the Newhaven boat trains, but as early as 1949 were occasionally supplanted by an electric locomotive, as seen on page 90.

Waterloo

The terminus which originally stood on the site of the present Waterloo opened in July 1848. It grew piecemeal, the last addition being made in 1885. By the end of the century, the station had become inadequate and so in 1900 work began on clearing the site for a new and larger terminus. In 1909 the first three platforms of the new Waterloo came into use, but it was not until 1922 that building ceased and Queen Mary could declare the station officially open. In the event, not quite all the old station was replaced, the 1885 addition being used for the Windsor line platforms, Nos 16 to 21.

I travelled daily to and from Waterloo during my second spell of commuting between 1962 and 1985. Thus in July 1967 I saw the last days of main-line steam services into London. How strange that the Southern, which had pioneered main-line electrification, should have provided these!

Kensington Olympia

The West London Railway from Willesden Junction to Kensington opened in 1844. It was extended south, across the Thames, to Clapham Junction in 1863 and then became an important north-south link. In 1869 Kensington station was rebuilt in LNWR style and renamed Addison Road. It was renamed again on 19 December 1946 as Kensington Olympia after the adjacent exhibition halls. The station is quite near to South Kensington and so as a student I sometimes went there by bus to watch and photograph the traffic. On 15 April 1950 I travelled south from Olympia on the first stage of a tour of London junctions arranged by the Stephenson Locomotive Society. The train was hauled by 'C' Class 0-6-0 No 31716.

Clapham Junction

It was in 1863 that a station serving the lines from Waterloo to Woking, Waterloo to Windsor, and Victoria to Brighton, and also the extended West London Railway from Willesden Junction, was opened at Clapham Junction. The station and nearby goods yards and carriage sidings came to occupy an enormous area.

In the days of steam, one saw all the main-line services from Waterloo to Bournemouth, Salisbury and Exeter, much of the traffic from Victoria, and goods trains from Willesden bound for Norwood Junction. These last were often hauled by Class 'W' 2-6-4Ts but sometimes by LMS engines, including ex-LNWR 0-8-0s and Stanier Class '8F' 2-8-0s (see pages 92–93). In addition one saw a great variety of engines shunting coaching stock and working empty trains to and from Waterloo. It is not surprising that both as a student and as an office worker I would sometimes break my journey to Town to take pictures.

Above right *'Baby Scot' Class '6P5F' 4-6-0 No 45503 The Royal Leicestershire Regiment in No 8 Platform at Euston on 15 June 1957.*

Right *Stanier two-cylinder 2-6-4T No 42611 waiting to take empty stock out of Platform 1 of the demolished Euston terminus at midday on 8 October 1963.*

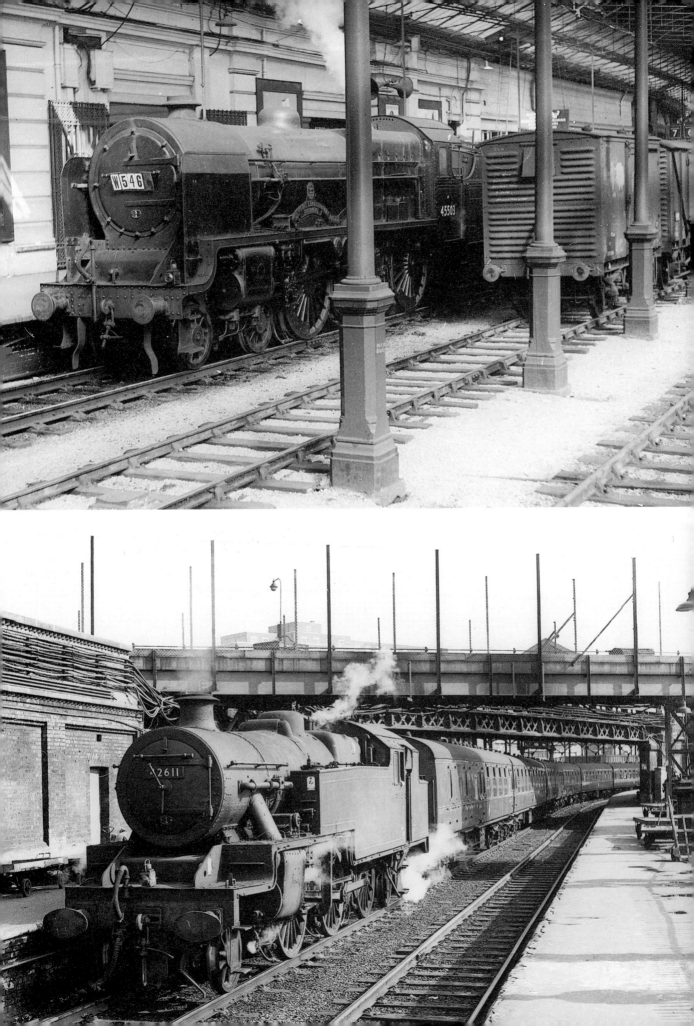

74 **Above** *'Pacific' No 46255* City of Hereford *in Euston on 30 June 1951.*

Below *Rebuilt 'Royal Scot' 4-6-0 No 46122* Royal Ulster Rifleman *on 'The Comet' express at Euston, 15 June 1957. I travelled to Manchester on this train to join a photographic excursion train to Windermere on the following day.*

Above *The sole British Railways Class '8P' 'Pacific',* No 71000 Duke of Gloucester, *at the departure side of Euston, 20 March 1957.* AD

Below *Desolation during the reconstruction of Euston, 8 October 1963.*

75

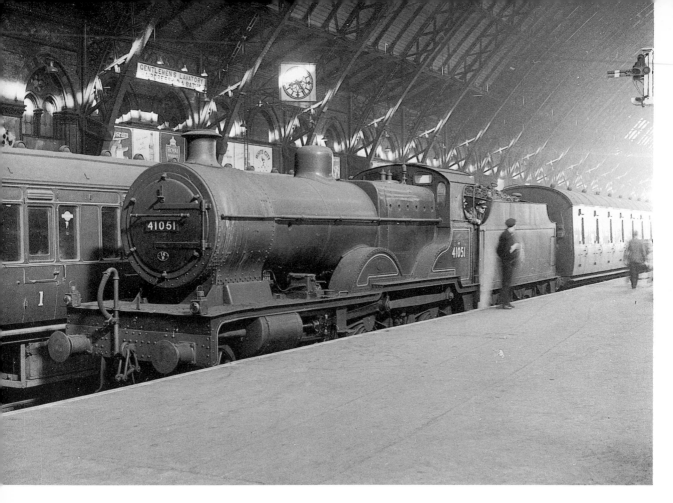

76   **Above** *Former LMS 'Compound' 4-4-0 No 41051 inside St Pancras, 1 July 1950.*   **Below** *Stanier 2-6-2T No 40155 at St Pancras, 25 March 1949.*

Above *'Jubilee' Class 4-6-0 No 45565* Victoria *entering St Pancras, 24 April 1951.* *AD*

Below *No 10000, the sole main line diesel-electric locomotive completed at Derby Works before nationalization, on the 2.15 pm train to Manchester at St Pancras in 1948.* *AD*

Above *Gresley Class 'A3' 'Pacific' No 61* Pretty Polly *at King's Cross at 1.40 pm on 30 September 1948.*

Below *Gresley 0-6-2Ts Nos 9522, Class 'N2', and 9441, Class 'N1', at the suburban side of King's Cross at 12.30 pm on 25 September 1948. Both engines have condensing apparatus for working in the Underground.*

Above *Two types of 'Pacific' inside King's Cross: No 60125* Scottish Union *of Class 'A1' and No 60055* Woolwinder *of Class 'A3'. 2 February 1959.* *AD*

Below *Class 'A1' 'Pacific' No 60120 (later named* Kittiwake*) at King's Cross in 1948 or 1949.* *AD* 79

Above *'B1' Class 4-6-0 No 1135, 'B12' 4-6-0 No 1523 and streamlined 'Sandringham', 'B17/5', Class 4-6-0 No 1670* City of London *in the locomotive yard, Liverpool Street, in 1948.* *AD*

Below *'Sandringham' Class 4-6-0 No 61609* Quidenham *at Liverpool Street in 1948.* *AD*

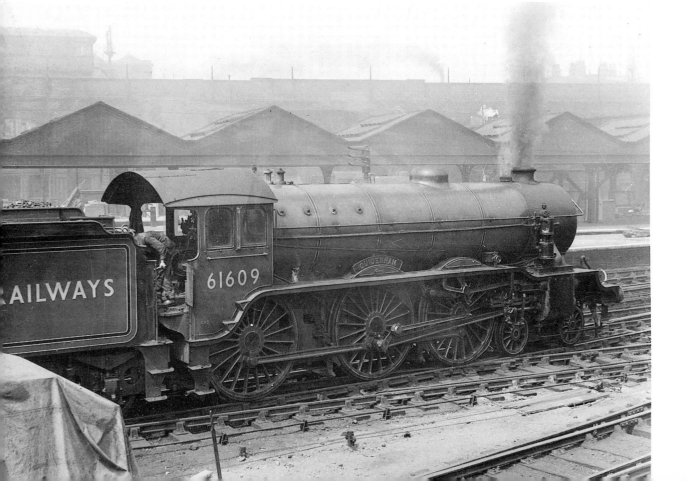

Above *'B1' 4-6-0 No 61109 at Liverpool Street about to depart for Norwich on the 'Norfolkman', 25 May 1957.*

Below *'Britannia' Class 'Pacific' No 70001 Lord Hurcomb at Liverpool Street on 18 April 1951.* *AD*

82   **Above** *Class 'A5' 4-6-2T No 69814 at Marylebone.* AD

Below *Thompson 'L1' Class 2-6-2T No 67726 at the coaling stage just outside Marylebone station at 3.40 pm on 27 August 1948.*

Above *An Inner Circle train at South Kensington on 12 September 1950 formed of Metropolitan stock renovated by London Transport in 1934. The doors were hand-operated.*

Below *Rush-hour trains at Moorgate on 31 May 1951. From left to right are former Metropolitan electric trains ('T' stock) in varnished wood livery, the 5.00 pm to New Barnet behind Gresley Class 'N2' 0-6-2T No 69580, and the 5.11 pm to St Albans behind Fowler Class '3' 2-6-2T No 40036.* AD

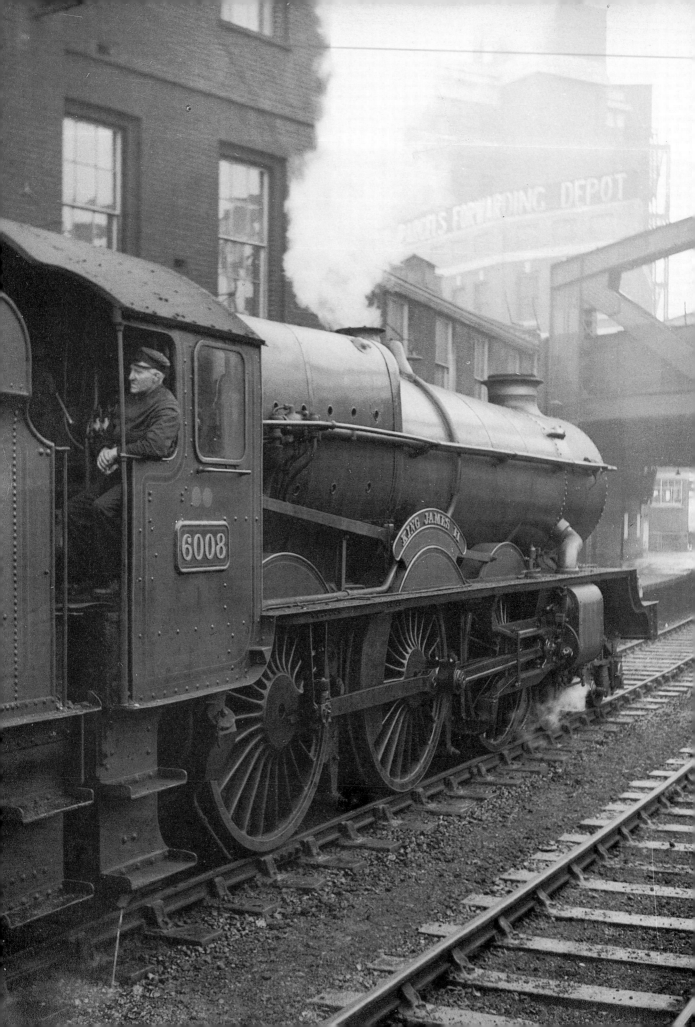

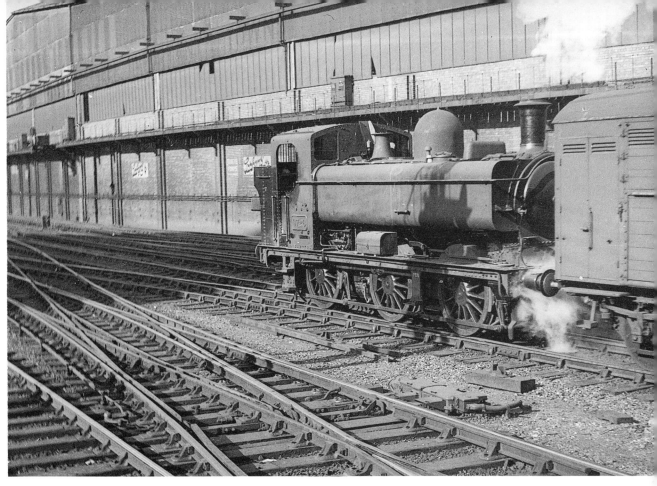

Left *'King' Class 4-6-0 No 6008* King James II *at Paddington on 13 November 1948.*

Above *'5700' Class pannier tank No 9726 at Paddington on 23 October 1948.*

Below *'Castle' Class 4-6-0 No 5063* Earl Baldwin *leaving Paddington on 13 November 1948.*

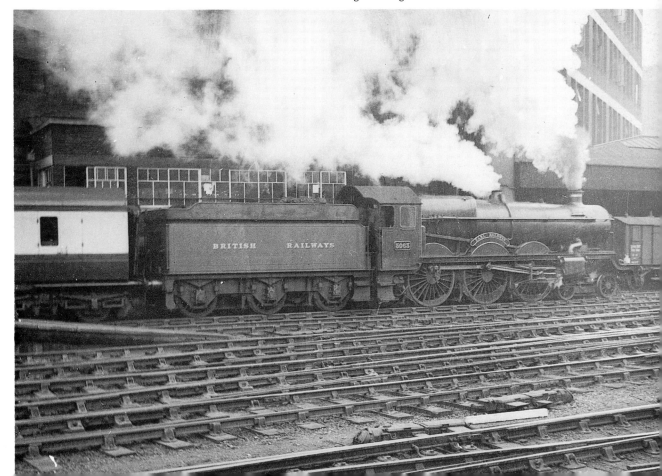

Above *Class 'H1' 'Atlantic' No 2038* Portland Bill entering London Bridge. *AD*

Below *Fairburn-design 2-6-4T No 42097 leaving London Bridge on 19 August 1950.* *AD*

Right *'West Country' 'Pacific' No 34096* Trevone *approaching London Bridge high level station on 17 June 1950.* *AD*

Above *'E2' Class 0-6-0T at the Eastern Section side of Victoria, one of the few Southern engines I was able to photograph in its pre-war livery. 26 July 1948.*

Below *Class 'H2' 'Atlantic' No 2421* South Foreland *at Victoria at 10.00 am on 20 November 1947.*

Above *'Schools' Class 4-4-0 No 926* Repton *in the Eastern Section of Victoria, the Continental side, on 9 February 1948.*

Below *'C2X' Class 0-6-0 goods engine No 32532 in the Central Section of Victoria on 17 January 1950. Notice the Southern Railway style of lettering.*

Above *Ex-LB&SCR 4-6-2T No 32326, Class 'J2', in Southern-style malachite green livery shunting at Victoria on 20 July 1949.*

Below *Electric locomotive No 20003 leaving Victoria at 9.35 am on 18 May 1959 with a Newhaven boat train. The leading carriage is in the smart red and cream livery of that era.*

Above *'Schools' Class 4-4-0 No 30905* Tonbridge *on our train for Tonbridge entering Waterloo (High Level) station on 18 April 1953.*

Below *An 'M7' 0-4-4T in Waterloo, having brought the empty 'Devon Belle' into the station. August 1951.*

91

Above *Former LNWR 0-8-0 No 49342 on a north-bound goods train at Kensington Olympia on 15 April 1950.*

Below *Riddles-design War Department 2-8-0 No 77030 on a southbound goods passing Kensington Olympia on the same day.*

Above *The 'Devon Belle' observation car on 8 June 1950 behind 'H' Class 0-4-4T No 31311. It was turned ready for its return journey by being taken to Kensington Olympia and back via opposite branches of the triangle junction at Clapham Junction.*

Below *A southbound freight train approaching Kensington Olympia hauled by 'W' Class 2-6-4T No 31916 on 8 June 1950.*

93

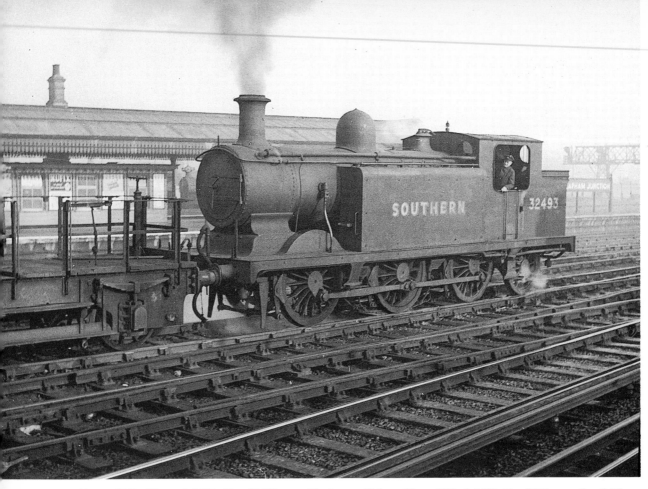

94

Above *'E4' Class 0-6-2T No 32493 at Clapham Junction, in Southern livery but with its number increased by 30000, on 16 February 1949.*

Below *Class 'I3' 4-4-2T No 2021 on the 9.08 am Victoria-Oxted-Tunbridge Wells train passing Clapham Junction on 25 October 1948.*

Above *Former LSWR 4-6-2T of Class 'H16', No 30520, at Clapham Junction on 1 April 1949. These engines were often used for empty stock workings into Waterloo.*

Below *Urie 'H15' Class 4-6-0 No 30510 on empty stock at Clapham Junction on 1 March 1963.*

Above *Class 'B1' 4-4-0 No 1443 at Clapham Junction on 5 October 1950.*

Below *Class 'M7' 0-4-4T No 30244 at the same location in lined malachite green livery with yellow lettering. 16 February 1949.*

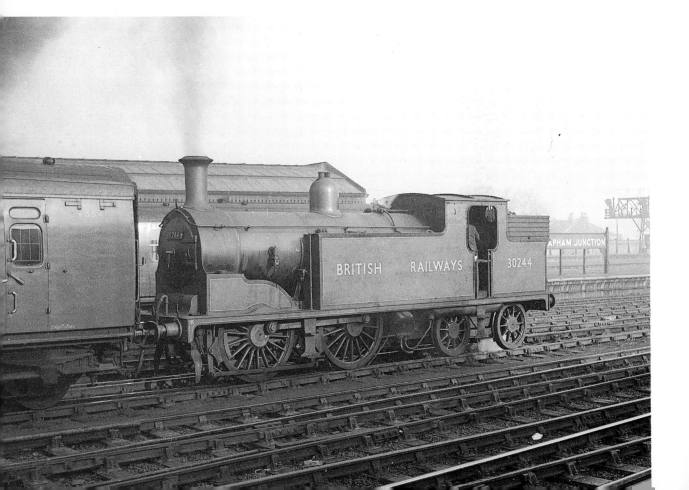

Above *Ex-LB&SCR 2-6-0 No 32345 of Class 'K' at Tattenham Corner on 4 June 1954. The engine was built to the design of L.B. Billinton, and was completed in December 1916.*

Below *Ex-L&SWR Drummond Class 'M7' 0-4-4T*

No 30675 (built at Nine Elms Works in 1897) with an ex-LMS parcels van and a horse-box at Epsom on 10 December 1955. It stands near the connection to the sidings for the goods platform adjacent to the station. The platform and southern siding were removed in the winter of 1980, the northern siding in December 1984.

97

Above left *Former SE&CR Wainwright Class 'D' 4-4-0 No 31488 passing the southern slope of Box Hill as it approaches Deepdene station, Dorking, on a Guildford train on 24 December 1954. This engine was built at Ashford in 1901.*

Left *Maunsell Class 'U' 2-6-0 No 31800 at Redhill shed on 14 September 1963. This engine was built at Brighton in 1926 as Class 'K' 2-6-4T No A800 River Cray, and was rebuilt as a tender engine in 1928. As may be seen by comparing this picture with that of No 31620 at Betchworth* **above** *the running plate is lower and the splashers are larger than for the engines built directly as Class 'U'.*

Above *Class 'U' 2-6-0 No 31620 (built at Ashford in 1928) approaching Betchworth station on a Redhill train on 4 July 1964.*

Right *Ex-GWR Churchward '4300' Class 2-6-0 No 5396 on a Reading train near Shere, 14 August 1954.*

Above *'Merchant Navy' Class 4-6-2 No 35030 — no longer carrying its name* Elder Dempster Lines *— at Vauxhall on 3 July 1967, during the last week of steam services into Waterloo.*

Below *A train from Kensington Olympia at Clapham Junction on 4 July 1967. The engine is a 2-6-2T of H.G. Ivatt's 1946 LMS design.*

Above *Former LNER Class 'J94' 0-6-0ST No 68013 (originally War Department No 75125, built by Hunslet of Leeds in 1944 and bought from the Ministry of Supply in 1946) shunting at Cromford near the foot of the Sheep Pasture incline of the Cromford & High Peak Line. Note the old locomotive tenders used for taking water for locomotives at Sheep Pasture Top and* *Middleton Top. 24 September 1962.* EDD

Below *The foot of the Sheep Pasture incline photographed by me on the same day. The lower part of a catch-pit for runaway wagons is just visible under the bridge. Notice the ex-LNWR signal with its corrugated arm.*

102

Left *A southbound Edinburgh-St Pancras express passing Ais Gill on 7 September 1954 headed by 'Jubilee' and Class '5' 4-6-0s.*

Below left *Class '5' No 44674 entering Kirkby Stephen West on the train by which we returned to Appleby during the evening of 4 September 1954 following our walk to Smardale.*

Right *Stanier Class '5' 4-6-0s Nos 45126 (pilot) and 44828 on a northbound Edinburgh express at Appleby on 3 September 1954.*

Below *Class '5' 4-6-0 No 45364 leaving Appleby on a local train during the evening of 6 September 1954.*

Above *Class 'J21' 0-6-0 No 65103 enters Appleby East on a Darlington train on the morning of Tuesday 7 September 1954.*

Below *A two-car diesel set forming a Darlington train at Appleby East on the morning of 8 September 1959. The leading car is No E50257, a Metropolitan Cammell motor brake second.*   *EDD*

104

Above *A Saltburn-Penrith excursion approaching Appleby East at about midday on Sunday 5 September 1954. The engine was 'J21' Class 0-6-0 No 65103; the rival photographer is my father.*

Below *British Railways Standard Class '3' 2-6-0 No 77001 passing the remains of Smardale station on a train of empty wagons. Smardale viaduct, in the background, carries the Settle-Carlisle line over Scandal Beck. 4 September 1954.*

Above *Ex-NER Worsdell 0-6-0, LNER Class 'J21', BR No 65103, approaching Kirkby Stephen East on a Penrith train during the evening of 31 August 1954.*

Below *British Railways Standard Class '2' 2-6-0 No 78019 at Kirkby Stephen East on a Darlington train. Taken at about 4.30 pm on Tuesday 31 August 1954.*

Above *A Fowler Class '3' 2-6-2T at Harrow and Wealdstone on the Stanmore Village branch train, 8 August 1953.*

Below *Fowler (LMS) design 2-6-2T No 40043 at Stanmore Village on 13 September 1952, the last day of the passenger service on the top end of the line, from Belmont to Stanmore.*

Above *'Princess Royal' Class 'Pacific' No 46204 Princess Louise on an up express between Hatch End and Headstone Lane on 20 February 1954. The locomotive is in the BR green livery.*

Below *Experimental three-car diesel unit at Harrow and Wealdstone on 11 April 1954. Built by British United Traction Co, it was used on the Belmont and Watford Junction-St Albans branches.*

Above *The famous locomotive* Royal Scot, *rebuilt and renumbered 46100 but still carrying the plates commemorating its exhibition in Chicago and 11,000-mile tour of the USA and Canada in 1933,* *heading a Euston express passing Watford Junction on 19 March 1955.*

Below *Class '5' No 44831 photographed from the footbridge at Watford Junction station, 19 March 1955.*

Above *Changing engines at Rickmansworth. Former Metropolitan Railway electric locomotive No 1, in grey livery, leaving the train it had brought from Baker Street on 27 March 1954.*

Below *Thompson Class 'L1' 2-6-4T comes on to the train ready to take it on to Aylesbury.*

Above *Former GCR Robinson 4-4-2T, LNER Class 'C13', leaving Chesham for Chalfont and Latimer during the afternoon of 27 March 1954.*

Below *Thompson LNER Class 'B1' 4-6-0 No 61186 at*

Pinner on a train for Marylebone, 7 March 1959. This picture was taken before the quadrupling of the lines between Harrow-on-the-Hill and Rickmansworth, a project started before the Second World War but only completed in June 1962.

Left *'Britannia' Standard Class '7' 'Pacific' on an up express for Euston near Bourne End on 18 August 1956.*

Below *Class '5' 4-6-0 No 45004 on an up stopping train near Bourne End on the same day.*

Above *Class 'E4' 0-6-2T No 2468 at Clapham Junction on 24 December 1948. This was then the only 'E4' with its original Billinton short smokebox and elegant chimney. When built in 1898 it was named* Midhurst.

Below *The same locomotive, as No 32468, at Clapham Junction after losing its original boiler and chimney and being repainted in British Railways lined black livery. 24 September 1949.*

113

4. DERBYSHIRE

Both as a child and as a young man, it was to Derbyshire that I went to see my grandparents and other members of the family. My father's parents lived in Derby and my mother's in Ambergate and, subsequently, Bakewell. All these journeys, as well as those to Appleby, began at St Pancras, so I came to know the old Midland main line through Leicester, or alternatively Oakham and Nottingham, to Derby better than any other. I used to sit at the right of the train because the goods lines and almost all the locomotive sheds were to the east of the passenger lines. Before the war this choice had the disadvantage of providing a less good view of Hendon aerodrome, with its silver Hawker 'Fury' and yellow Hawker 'Hart', biplanes, and the Handley-Page aerodrome at Radlett, with its four-engined biplane airliners of the 'Hannibal' class. This mention of aircraft reminds me of the occasion in March 1937 when, on a journey to Derby, we had a magnificent view of a twin-engined high-wing monoplane bomber flying very low towards the train. We were delayed at Leicester and learned that the plane had torn open the roof of the kitchen car and crash landed in a field beside the line. The delay was caused by the damaged car being taken out of the train.

A journey to Derby provided a feast of engines. To give an idea of the menu, I summarize what I noted on a journey by the 8.30 am train on 19 August 1944:

'Jubilee'	4-6-0	9
Class '5'	4-6-0	3
'Compound'	4-4-0	7
Class '3P'	4-4-0	3
Class '2P'	4-4-0	8
Class '1P'	2-4-0	1
Class '8F'	2-8-0	16
Class '7F'	0-8-0	3
Class '6F'	0-8-0	1
Class '5F'	2-6-0	4
Class '4F'	0-6-0	19
Class '3F'	0-6-0	22
Class '2F'	0-6-0	1
Garratt	2-6-0 + 0-6-2	5
Class '4P'	2-6-4T	11
Class '3P'	2-6-2T	13
Class '1P'	0-4-4T	9
Class '3F'	0-6-0T	8
Class '1F'	0-6-0T	8
WD	2-10-0	7
WD	2-8-0	2
USA	2-8-0	2
SR ('700')	0-6-0	1
LNER ('N1')	0-6-2T	1
	Total	164

The rarest of these engines was the Midland Class '1P' 2-4-0 No 20216 which lived at Kettering shed.

Derby became an important railway centre because three early companies built lines which terminated there. These companies were the Midland Counties Railway, which opened its line to Nottingham in June 1839; the Birmingham & Derby Junction Railway, opened in August 1839; and the North Midland Railway, which opened a route to Masborough, and then on to Leeds, in 1840. These were the companies which amalgamated in 1844 to form the Midland Railway. The new company expanded the railway works which had already been established in Derby and made the town its centre for the manufacture and repair of locomotives, rolling-stock and signalling equipment.

My grandfather, Arthur Davenport senior, was well known in the Carriage and Wagon Works and took me there before the war. My clearest memories are, not surprisingly, of the more spectacular items: a circular saw, by no means well guarded, with a blade of a diameter considerably more than the height of a man; and a little corrugated iron shanty in which a man, with the aid of a deafening steam jet, bent strips of wood to the profile of a carriage roof. I also remember a mock-up of

Left *'Jubilee' Class 4-6-0 No 5652* Hawke *on the bridge over the river Derwent just north of Derby station at 4.45 pm on 27 March 1948.*

a complete carriage compartment.

There were three excellent places for watching trains in Derby: the station; the footpath at the side of the railway bridge over the river Derwent; and the bridge carrying London Road over the line to Birmingham and the lines into the Carriage and Wagon Works. One needed binoculars to read numbers clearly from the third of these viewpoints, and so for photography the other two were best.

At the time of my visits to relatives, Derby station was still very much as it had been when built in 1839-40 for the North Midland Railway. The roof was carried by slender iron columns (see page 118), and there was a lattice iron footbridge which linked the platforms and then continued over more lines to the Locomotive Works. The steps up from the platforms were of cast iron with square cells in the treads into which little blocks of hard wood had been set. The risers were liberally adorned with enamel 'Mazawattee Tea' signs.

Between 1952 and 1954 the character of the station was completely changed when the overall roof, bridge and platforms were replaced with structures mainly of concrete (see page 122). The new bridge was covered in, and the platforms had separate canopies. The massive, but dignified, brick and stone station buildings have been replaced, despite protest, only recently.

London Road bridge gave a panoramic view of the lines to Birmingham and London, the Locomotive Works and the motive power depot. The sidings between the lines to London and No 4 Shed were filled with engines, some awaiting repair and others just out of the Works. Many had been 'soled and heeled' — that is, given a minor repair and sent out with a repainted smoke box and chimney and with cleaned and varnished numbering and lettering. What was so interesting was the fact that engines were sent to Derby Works from far afield, so that one saw members of classes that one would otherwise never have seen. On 30 August 1945 I saw one of the 2-8-0s, built by the Midland Railway for the Somerset & Dorset Joint Railway, No 13801. On 23 September the following year, I saw No 7191, a Sentinel shunter.

A selection of LMS and LNER tickets relating to Derby.

It was in 1944 that I started to take an interest in the LNER route from Nottingham through Derby (Friargate) to Burton-on-Trent or Tutbury. The necessary branch from Ilkeston, north of Nottingham, to Egginton Junction on the North Staffordshire Railway had been opened by the Great Northern in 1878 as a deliberate intrusion into Midland Railway territory. The passenger services west of Derby were withdrawn in December 1939 and never reinstated. The services between Nottingham and Derby survived until September 1964. My first journey on the line was on 10 April 1945 from Breadsall to Derby behind ex-GNR 4-4-0 No 3048 of Class 'D2'. Later that year I twice travelled from Friargate to Nottingham (Victoria) and back, being hauled on the outward journey of the second visit, on 5 September, by a most unusual engine far from its original home — ex-Metropolitan Railway 4-4-4T, LNER No 6422, Class 'H2'. How I wish I could have photographed this and the many other interesting LNER locomotives, of 20 different classes, that I saw during those visits and my last visit of all, on 1 August 1946. Most notable amongst the engines I saw at Nottingham were the 'B8' 4-6-0 *Glenalmond* and one of the elegant class 'C4' 'Atlantics', No 6091, both of Great Central origin. Some consolation came to me in 1948 when I was able to photograph one of the last 'H2s' at Stratford (see page 173).

In going to see my grandparents at Ambergate or, later on, Bakewell, it was necessary to take a Derby to Manchester (page 121), 'Compound' and Class '2P' stopping train because the expresses usually called only at Matlock and Millers Dale. These stopping trains were hauled by second-string locomotives including Horwich 2-6-0s 4-4-0s, 2-6-4Ts and sometimes even an 0-6-0 goods engine. I was very young when visiting Ambergate but I do remember, after a journey on the Clay Cross and Chesterfield line, having to step across the quite enormous gap between the carriage and the strongly curved, wooden-slatted platform at the north side of the triangular station.

The most intriguing stretch of the journey to Bakewell was a mile and a half beyond Whatstandwell station where, at High Peak Junction, a single line branched off and ran away out of sight, along the wooded slope of the Derwent Valley. It soon reappeared, just across the Cromford Canal, where there was a wharf and a goods shed near the foot of a rope-worked incline. Moments later one saw, high up a hillside and silhouetted against the sky, an old LNWR signal. These were the beginnings of the Cromford & High Peak Railway, one of the oldest and most unusual mineral lines in the country.

Originally the C&HPR was 33 miles long, the first 15½ miles to Hurdlow being opened in May 1830 and the remainder, to Whaley Bridge, in July 1831. There were eight rope-worked inclines. In 1853 the connection with the Midland Railway at High Peak Junction was made, and four years later the northern end of the line at Whaley Bridge was connected to a line from Stockport. A central stretch between Parsley Hay and Ladmanlow was realigned by 1892. At the same time, a portion which ran north from Landmanlow to

Shallcross was abandoned. Much of the realigned stretch, from Parsley Hay to Hindlow, was doubled by 1894 and was incorporated in a route completed five years later from Ashbourne to Buxton.

Remarkably, passenger services were available over the C&HPR during the period 1833 to 1876, the passengers being supposed to walk the numerous rope-worked inclines. The latter were progressively reduced in number by combination, realignment of the line, and closure of the northern section, so that by 1892 there remained only the Sheep Pasture and Middleton inclines between Cromford and Parsley Hay.

My father and I twice visited the Cromford & High Peak line from Derby soon after the war, in July and September 1946. On our second visit he photographed the little ex-LNWR 2-4-0 which worked the mile and a half of track between the top of the Sheep Pasture and the bottom of the Middleton incline, and also the ex-North London Railway 0-6-0Ts 27515 and 27530 shedded at Middleton Top for working the rest of the line (see page 124). We explored the route more thoroughly, from Rowsley, in September 1962, and were shown the famous fish-bellied cast iron rails, bearing the initials C&HPR, inside the workshop at Cromford. At this time the outer sections of the line were worked by ex-War Department 0-6-0STs (see page 125), and the section between the inclines by Stanier-Kitson 0-4-0ST No 47007 (see page 125). We saw for the first time a train on the famous Hopton incline which, at its steepest, had a gradient of 1 in 14. Unfortunately, the train was going down, not up, so we missed what must have been one of the most spectacular of all steam workings.

118   **Above** *Class '3P' 4-4-0 No 756 at the south end of Derby Station on 26 March 1948.*

Below *Class '5' 4-6-0 No 4788, bearing the attractive sans serif lettering introduced in 1946 on cab and tender, at the south end of Derby station at 11.15 am on 1 April 1948.*

Above *Class '2P' 4-4-0 No 411 at the north end of Derby station, at 11.30 am on 1 April 1948.*

Below *Johnson Class '1P' 0-4-4T No 1397 at the north end of Derby station on 27 March 1948.*

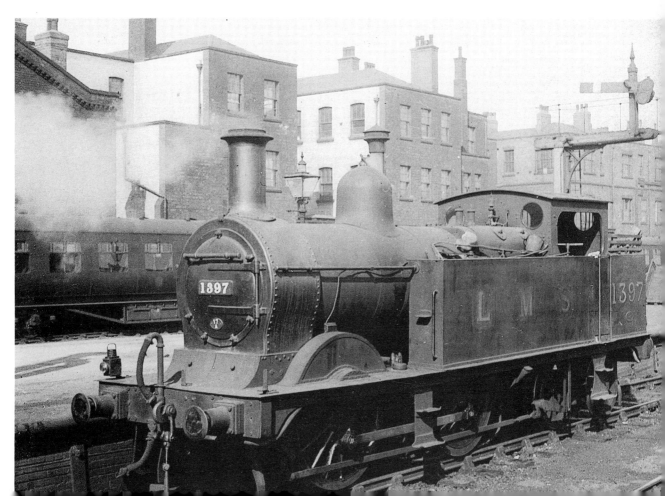

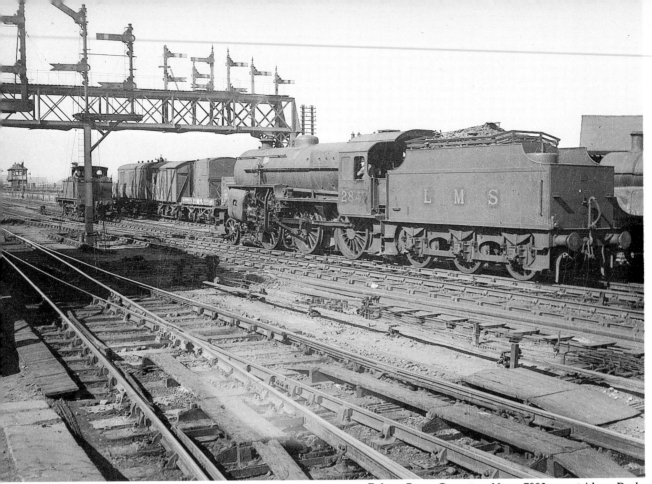

Above *Hughes '5F' 2-6-0 No 2847 at the north end of Derby station. Notice the '1F' 0-6-0T in the distance with its backless cab.* *AD*

120

Below *Beyer-Garratt No 7992 outside Derby Locomotive Works, at 5.30 pm on 30 March 1948. These engines did not normally work to Derby, so this member of the class had presumably come to the Works for attention.*

Above *Stanier Class '5' 4-6-0 No 44851 on an up express approaching Breadsall level crossing on 22 April 1959.*   *AD*

Below *The 12.54 pm train to Derby entering Bakewell station behind Class '5F' 2-6-0 No 42872. 9 June 1954.*   *AD*

122 **Above** *A Fowler Class '4F' 0-6-0 goods engine at Derby station on 9 June 1954 during the reconstruction.* AD

Below *A Stanier Class '8F' 2-8-0 passing between Derby Works and station at 5.20 pm on 30 March 1948. The shadow of the engine on the parcels van shows how low the sun was.*

Above *Robinson 'Large Director' Class 4-4-0, LNER classification 'D11/1', No 62667* Somme, *from Lincoln shed, at the north end of Derby station on a Nottingham and Lincoln train. 20 July 1954.* AD

Below *Ex-GNR 4-4-0, LNER Class 'D2', No 2161 at Derby on its way to Nottingham Victoria. 5 May 1950.* AD

Above *Ex-NLR 0-6-0T No 27530 (later BR No 58862) outside the engine shed near the top of the Middleton incline, C&HPR, on 27 September 1946.* *AD*

Below *Another ex-NLR 0-6-0T at Cromford near the foot of the Sheep Pasture incline on 20 April 1953. This engine, seen as BR No 58850, was LMS No 27505 and is now, most happily, preserved on the Bluebell Railway.* *AD*

Above *Stanier-Kitson 0-4-0ST No 47007 at the top of the Sheep Pasture incline on 25 September 1962.*

Below *War Department-design 0-6-0ST No 68012, LNER Class 'J94', taking a train down the famous Hopton incline which, at its steepest, had a gradient of 1 in 14. 24 September 1962.*

5. APPLEBY IN WESTMORLAND

The Royal and Ancient Borough of Appleby stands on the River Eden three miles west of the green fells of the Pennine Chain. It is a quiet and beautiful place with a broad main street, Boroughgate, which runs from the Church of St Lawrence past the black and white Moot Hall and then, tree-lined, up to the gates of the castle. It used to be the county town of Westmorland, and until October 1970 the assizes were held there. When Westmorland disappeared in 1974, through combination with Cumberland to form the new county of Cumbria, its name was perpetuated by linkage with that of Appleby.

Across the river from Boroughgate and high up the side of the valley run two railways. One is the once threatened, but recently reprieved, Settle to Carlisle line built to provide the Midland Railway with an independent route from London to Scotland. The other is a vestige of the first railway to arrive at Appleby, the North Eastern Railway Eden Valley branch, which ran from Kirkby Stephen to a junction with the London & North Western Railway at Clifton, just south of Penrith.

The Eden Valley branch was an offshoot of an important mineral route built by the South Durham & Lancashire Union Railway — a subsidiary of the famous Stockton & Darlington Railway — between West Auckland and Tebay. Via this route, opened in 1861, coke was taken westwards from Durham to ironworks in Cumberland and Furness, and iron ore was taken eastwards to ironworks in County Durham. Between Bowes and Barras the line crossed Stainmore Summit (at 1,370 feet above sea level the

highest point on a railway in England) before dropping down to Kirkby Stephen. The branch from there through Appleby to Clifton was opened on 8 April 1862, but the connection faced south so did not allow trains to run north into Penrith. A new connection enabling trains to do this was opened on 1 August 1863, a day which was, as it happened, only two weeks after that on which the Stockton & Darlington Railway amalgamated with the North Eastern.

It was the building, between 1869 and 1876, of the Settle–Carlisle line that brought my great grandfather, Thomas Woodward, to Appleby where he lived whilst superintending the signalling. His daughter Alice had been born in 1870 and so spent her early years at Appleby. After her marriage to my grandfather, Arthur Davenport, she evidently convinced him of the place's charms because they spent a number of holidays there. Thus it came about that their son, my father, was infected with an enthusiasm for Appleby at an early age. He clearly remembered seeing the first Midland Compound 4-4-0s (Nos 2631 and 2632) there when newly introduced. This must have been in 1902, when he was eight. Those Johnson engines did not look like the later Deeley and Fowler 'Compounds', having box-like extensions to the cab to serve as the rear wheel splashers, and large tenders carried by a pair of four-wheel bogies.

My own love of Appleby was nurtured during five holidays between the years 1933 and 1939. The most noteworthy railway event of those visits, and the one which I remember best, was on 16 August 1938 when my father took me to Penrith to see the northbound 'Coronation Scot'. We travelled there behind LNER Class 'E4' 2-4-0 No 7411, one of the ex-Great Eastern Railway 'Intermediate' Class engines which had been fitted with a side-window cab to help the enginemen withstand the fierce North Country winters (see page

Left A fine display of smoke from '4F' 0-6-0 No 44572 as it pulls its train from the connection between the former LMS and LNER lines just north of Appleby West station. 24 August 1956.   AD

179). The 'Coronation Scot' duly appeared, passing quite slowly round the curve through the station. It was hauled by streamlined 'Pacific' No 6224 *Princess Alexandra* in its elegant livery, matching that of the train, of a medium blue with longitudinal white (*not* silver) lines at carriage window level. Another interesting engine we saw at Penrith was ex-Glasgow & South Western Railway 0-6-2T No 16911.

Some years we travelled to Appleby via my grandparents' home in Derby, but usually we left St Pancras in style at 10 am in the 'Thames-Clyde Express'. The pleasure of the journey was enhanced by luncheon in the dining car. How I wish I had the recipe of the LMS tomato soup which was less lurid in shade and more interesting in both texture and flavour than the present-day tinned commodity! At Leeds (City), a terminus, the train had to reverse, a new engine being attached to the rear. The Midland station was beside that used by the LNER where one usually saw a 'Hunt' or 'Shire' 4-4-0 in its beautiful apple green livery.

Thirty-six miles from Leeds one reached Hellifield, with its glimpses of Lancashire & Yorkshire Railway engines, and three miles further on, the beginning of the Settle to Carlisle line. A climb of 15 miles, nearly all at 1 in 100, brought the train to Blea Moor tunnel, whence a ten-mile stretch with no severe gradient led through Garsdale, junction for the Hawes branch, to the summit of the line, 1,169 feet above sea level, at Ais Gill. A rapid descent of 17 miles, much at 1 in 100, was all that was needed to reach Appleby. As a lover of limestone country with its green mountains and its patchwork of stone-walled fields, I can think of no route more beautiful, and I was delighted when, in April 1989, the Transport Secretary, Mr Channon, refused British Rail permission to close it.

To step from a warm railway carriage into keen North Country air, with its subtle fragrance, was a marvellous start to a holiday. The feeling of exhilaration, usually heightened by a roar of steam from the engine, made one realize anew that, physically speaking, one does not live in Surrey; one merely exists.

In steam days, Appleby was a remarkable place for watching and photographing trains.

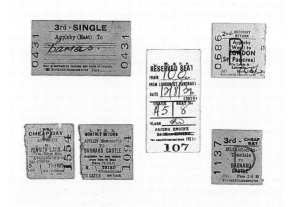

A collection of tickets relating to Appleby.

There were many fine viewpoints, the LMS and LNER stations and the bridges carrying the road to Hilton over the two lines being particularly good. Just north of the LMS bridge was, and probably still is, the Express Dairy depot. Express trains used to stop here so that milk tank wagons from the siding could be attached at the rear. The dairy took its name from this sensible method of supplying London with fresh north country milk.

Between the two bridges just mentioned is a third over a cutting through which it was intended that North Eastern Railway trains should run into the Midland Railway station. This plan never materialized, and the LNER, and subsequently British Railways, maintained a separate station until the withdrawal of passenger services on 22 January 1962. In BR days it was called Appleby East to distinguish it from the former LMS station, Appleby West.

It was impossible, and fortunately unnecessary, to choose between the attractions of the two lines through Appleby. The Settle-Carlisle had the Scotch expresses, hauled by 'Jubilee', 'Baby Scot', Class '5' and, later, rebuilt 'Royal Scot' 4-6-0s, and imposing goods trains behind '8F' 2-8-0s, '5F' 2-6-0s and '4F' 0-6-0s. The Eden Valley branch was a charming period piece with only a few passenger trains each way per day and even less goods activity. During my first post-war visit to Appleby, in 1947, all the trains were hauled by ex-North Eastern Railway 0-6-0 tender engines. Usually, the 5 ft 1¼ in

'J21s' worked the passenger trains and the 4 ft 7½ in 'J25s' (page 134) the goods. By the time of my next holiday, 1954, Class '2' 2-6-0s, both of the LMS design and of the British Railways equivalent type, had started to replace these. My parents visited Appleby in 1955, 1956 and 1959, and their pictures show the arrival of the larger Class '3' 2-6-2Ts on the passenger trains. By 1959 the services had been taken over by diesel multiple units (see page 104).

The most pleasant way of savouring the Eden Valley branch was to travel from Appleby to Kirkby Stephen and back. At Kirkby Stephen one saw the traffic on the Tebay line and, just by the station, the locomotive shed. The journey, along the foot of the Pennines, provided a feast of good scenery and a sensation of travel quite different from that on a main line. Instead of the well-known 'de de de dum, de de de dum, de de de dum' of those days, the ancient carriages and short tails went 'clumpety, clumpety, clumpety', and gave a pleasantly erroneous impression of speed.

Between Kirkby Stephen and Crosby Garrett stations, the Settle–Carlisle line crosses the wooded valley of Scandal Beck by the ten-span Smardale Viaduct. On the southern slope was a single line which was, of course, the Tebay branch. We always hoped that one day, during a journey to or from Appleby, we should see a train in this beautiful setting. We never did. However, what we failed to do by accident, we twice managed to do by design. On 2 July 1951 my father and I went to Tebay by bus — for lack of a suitable train service — but were able to return to Kirkby Stephen and then Appleby by train. At Tebay we saw traffic on the Euston–Carlisle main line. Of special interest were some of the few Fowler Class '4P' 2-6-4Ts to be fitted with side-window cabs (see page 143). These engines were used for banking trains up Shap.

Our second view of the Tebay line was on 4 September 1954 when we travelled to Kirkby Stephen East by train and then walked to a bridge over the line near the remains of Smardale station — the normal passenger services to Tebay had been withdrawn on 1 December 1952. We were rewarded by the sight of a train of empty wagons hauled by the second of the BR Standard Class '3' 2-6-0s, No 77001. We ended our walk at Kirkby Stephen West whence we returned to Appleby behind Class '5' No 44674 in a train of two carriages, two vans and a milk tank.

In 1951 the timetable allowed an afternoon visit to Penrith, and this we made on 5 July. The most interesting engines there were the Webb 'Cauliflower' 0-6-0s (see page 138). In 1954 the train times were less convenient and all our journeys from Appleby East were southwards to Kirkby Stephen or beyond. On 3 September we went to Barras and so enjoyed a ride over Bouch's spindly Beelah Viaduct. This was large enough to be seen with the naked eye from Brackenber Moor (near Appleby), eight miles away. Three days later we went to Barnard Castle and so travelled over Stainmore summit as well. From Barnard Castle we made a return trip over the branch to Middleton-in-Teesdale in decidedly wet weather (see page 141).

My last holiday at Appleby was with my father, mother and sister in 1970. The railway scene had changed completely, all trains being hauled by diesel-electric locomotives. However, I did enjoy one quite unexpected and remarkable experience. I fell into conversation with the crew of a goods train at the old LNER station and they invited me for a ride in the brake van during their trip to collect stone from the quarry at Merrygill. Naturally I accepted and so enjoyed a grandstand view of the beautiful Pennine scenery, and the tragic remains of the closed stations. The guard told me that if the load became less than so many wagons per week (I think it was 20) the line would be closed. Closure did take place, on 3 November 1975, and all that remains now is the six-mile stretch from the junction just north of Appleby West to Warcop, retained because of the Ministry of Defence ranges nearby.

Above *An up Scotch express passing Appleby in August 1927. A class '2P' 4-4-0 pilots a three-cylinder compound.* AD

Below *An up Scotch express standing in Appleby station in August 1933. The train engine, 'Patriot', or popularly 'Baby Scot', Class 4-6-0 No 5992, was later renumbered 5515 and named* Caernarvon. *The pilot is a class '2P' 4-4-0.* AD

Above *The up 'Thames-Clyde Express' passing Appleby hauled by Class '5' 4-6-0 No 44856 and rebuilt 'Royal Scot' No 46109* Royal Engineer *at about 12.45 pm on 3 July 1951.*

Below *Class '5' No 44728 enters Appleby on a stopping train from the north at about 1.00 pm on 6 July 1951.*

132　**Above** *Fowler Class '4' compound 4-4-0 No 41129, with a nice early pattern of chimney, entering Appleby at 1.20 pm on Saturday 7 July 1951 on a Hellifield-Carlisle stopping train. Note the adjacent BR and LMS coach liveries.*

Below *Appleby station signal box, of characteristic Midland Railway design, on 1 July 1951.*

Above *'Britannia' Class 'Pacific' No 70016* Ariel *on a down express approaching Appleby on 5 July 1951. It was due to leave Appleby at 12.34 pm.*

Below *Hughes Class '5F' 2-6-0 No 42833 pilots 'Jubilee' 4-6-0 No 45632* Tonga *on a goods train approaching the Express Dairy depot at Appleby. 6.30 pm, 3 July 1951.*

Above *A southbound goods train entering Appleby NER station behind 'J25' 0-6-0 goods No 5695 on 11 September 1947.*
AD

Below *'J21' Class 0-6-0 No 5119 approaching Appleby from Penrith in September 1947.*
AD

Above *The Sunday excursion train from Saltburn and Redcar to Penrith (for Ullswater) on 1 July 1951. The engine was 'J21' Class 0-6-0 No 65090 and had left Appleby at 11.58 am.*

Below *Darlington-built Ivatt-design Class '2' 2-6-0 No 46467 at Appleby East on 6 July 1951, on the 11.02 train to Kirkby Stephen.*

'J21' Class 0-6-0 No 65033 approaching Appleby on the
6.08 pm train to Penrith, 3 July 1951.

'J25' Class 0-6-0 No 65655 at the same place makes heavier weather of the 1 in 100 climb than did No 65033. 6 July 1951.

Above *Class 'J21' 0-6-0 No 65033 on a Kirkby Stephen train in Penrith station, 5 July 1951.*

Below *'Cauliflower' Class 0-6-0 goods engine No 58396, at Penrith on the same day.*

Above *'J21' No 65033 enters Kirkby Stephen station on the Penrith train on the second part of our journey from Tebay to Appleby on 2 July 1951.*

Below *The prototype 'Deltic' diesel-electric locomotive passing the Express Dairy depot at Appleby on 28 August 1956. It was painted blue with yellow decorative lining.* AD

139

140

Left *Kirkby Stephen LNER station on 11 September 1947.* AD

Below left *Just to the east of Kirkby Stephen station on the same day. The engine on the left is 'J21' Class No 5032; that on the right is a 'J25'.* AD

Right *An eastbound goods leaving Barnard Castle hauled by Class '2' 2-6-0 No 78106 and another Class '2' 2-6-0, almost certainly of the Ivatt design. 6 September 1954.*

Below *Class 'G5' 0-4-4T No 67284 at Middleton-in-Teesdale during the wet afternoon of the same day. The branch closed on 30 November 1964.*

141

Left *'J21' Class No 65090 on its one-coach train to Kirkby Stephen waiting to leave Tebay, on the afternoon of 2 July 1951. The branch closed to passengers on 1 December 1952, while Tebay London Midland Region station closed on 1 July 1968.* AD

Above *A variant of the usual Fowler-design Class '4P' 2-6-4T. No 42404 is one of the 30 engines (Nos 42395 to 42424) which were fitted with side-window cabs. It is seen on 2 July 1951 in Tebay station and was used for banking goods trains up the notorious Shap incline where, in winter, the warmer cab would have been welcome.*

Below *Class 'A3' 'Pacific' No 95 Flamingo at Carlisle Citadel station on a running-in turn in beautiful LNER apple green livery on 9 September 1947.* AD

6. WHITBY

I was twice taken to Scarborough for seaside holidays before the war, but confess that my only clear railway memories from these are of the 15 in gauge North Bay Railway, with its petrol-driven engine based on a Gresley 'Pacific', and of the nearby 'water-chute'. My detailed recollections of railways in the North Yorkshire Moors area date from 1949 when my parents and I spent our summer holiday at Whitby.

The first railway there was the horse- and gravity-worked Whitby and Pickering line, opened for its full length of 24 miles on 26 May 1836. The route included a rope-worked incline 1,500 yards long and having a gradient, at its steepest, of 1 in 10. Because the line cost much more than the estimated sum to build, and because the handsome profits expected from stone and mineral traffic did not materialize, the undertaking struggled financially throughout its independent existence. This latter ended in 1844 when the line was bought by the York & North Midland Railway.

It was in July 1845 that the Whitby–Pickering line became joined to the national railway network through the opening by the York & North Midland of a main line from York to Scarborough and of a branch from Rillington, on the new line, to Pickering. However, it was not until 1865 — by which time the North Midland had, in 1854, become part of the North Eastern Railway — that steam trains could run right through to Whitby. This was made possible by the construction of a 4½ mile-long deviation bypassing the old incline.

That same year, 1865, a second rail route to Whitby was opened upon completion of a line running eastwards from Castleton, along the Esk Valley, to a junction with the Pickering to Whitby line at Grosmont.

The third railway to serve Whitby was the coast line from Middlesbrough to Scarborough. This was not the result of a single enterprise but was built in two stages by separate companies. The Whitby, Redcar & Middlesbrough Union Railway opened its line from Loftus to Whitby Town on 3 December 1883. It provided Whitby with a second station, Whitby West Cliff, rather less than half a mile to the north-west of Whitby Town. Between the two stations the line dropped down into the Esk valley, swinging right round so as to be facing north when it joined the line from Pickering at Bog Hall, half a mile south of the terminus.

The second stage was built by the Scarborough & Whitby Railway and was opened on 16 July 1885. The line had to cross the Esk Valley and did so by Larpool viaduct, a 13-arch brick structure 915 feet long and 125 feet high, measured from river bed to parapet (see page 151). The second arch, from the northern end, spanned what had become the connection between the new coastal route and the old line along the valley. That line was spanned by the fourth arch.

Larpool was not the only viaduct on the Scarborough–Middlesbrough route. There were five metal structures, having braced tubular supports, four of them between Whitby West Cliff and the next station, Sandsend (see page 150). The fifth, and largest, at Staithes — three stations beyond Sandsend — was 790 feet long and 125 feet high (see page 154).

Some Whitby area tickets.

Left *Class 'A8' 'Pacific' No 69858 in Whitby Town station in August 1949.*   *AD*

For our 1949 holiday we travelled on 8 August by train from King's Cross, changing at Grantham and York. The first stage of this journey was in the 'Flying Scotsman' behind 'A3' 'Pacific' No 60053 *Sansovino*; the second was behind 'A4' 'Pacific' No 60007 *Sir Nigel Gresley*; and the third was behind 'D49/2' 4-4-0 No 62759 *The Craven*. We were struck by the beauty of the scenery from Pickering onwards. Newtondale, the valley along which the line passes, is unspoiled by development because the main Pickering–Whitby road is nowhere near the railway but traverses the moorland above the valley to the east. Happily, thanks to the efforts of the North Yorkshire Moors Railway Preservation Society, one can still travel from Pickering to Grosmont by steam train.

Our hotel in Whitby was near the West Cliff station and we travelled by rail as often as we could, even when the journey was just to the centre of town. In readiness for the holiday we had obtained permits to visit both Whitby and Scarborough motive power depots. Although our visit to Whitby shed was photographically well worthwhile, it was less necessary to have a permit there than for most sheds because a road runs along to the west of the railway which gave a magnificent view of the locomotive yard with, in the background, the squat-towered church and the abbey ruins (see page 148).

We visited Scarborough twice and the spectacular coastal scenery, especially during the climb from Robin Hood's Bay to Ravenscar (page 151) was, in its very different way, as memorable as Newtondale. Scarborough shed was a large one by the main line to York. One of my rare invitations on to the footplate was to ride from there on 'A8' 'Pacific' tank No 69873 into Scarborough station (see page 156). All our journeys on the coast line were behind engines of this class, but we also saw, and photographed, 'A5' 4-6-2 tanks of Great Central design. Our journeys inland had more varied motive power, including 'G5' 0-4-4Ts 67272 and 7332, the 'A8' 69865 and 'D49' 4-4-0 No 62759 *The Craven*. Goods traffic was handled by Class 'J24' 0-6-0 tender engines.

This splendid holiday ended on 22 August.

We were hauled to York in the 9.25 train by another 'Hunt' Class locomotive, No 62726 *The Meynell* (page 153) and then, after a visit to the old York Railway Museum, returned to London behind the Peppercorn Class 'A1' 'Pacific' No 60127 in blue livery.

My next visit to Whitby was alone, and, I hesitate to admit, by car. In September 1962 I worked my way from home up eastern England staying briefly at interesting places, the first being King's Lynn and the second Goathland, where I stayed for four days. On the 19th I photographed Whitby Town station and then Whitby West Cliff, closed on 3 May 1958 but intact except for the removal of signals. I went to look at the junction for the Scarborough line at Prospect Hill and saw a DMU on its way to the Larpool viaduct. The Scarborough service survived until 6 March 1965.

On 20 September I visited the Roman road on Wheeldale moor, and on my way back called to have a look at Egton station. I had just taken one picture when I heard a locomotive whistle and was alerted soon enough to be able to photograph 'Q6' 0-8-0 on a short goods train heading for Whitby. The weather was improving and so I followed by car and was able to take further pictures of this fine North Eastern engine in sunshine at the goods yard near the Bog Hall level crossing (see page 155).

On the following day I gave my car a rest and visited Pickering by train. I was hauled by BR Standard Class '3' 2-6-2T No 82029, a locomotive much in evidence during that short holiday (see page 157).

My next visit to the North Yorkshire Moors was a fleeting one on 28 August 1972, made by car from York. We saw much of the stock of the NYMR at Grosmont station, but could not enjoy a ride on the line because at that time only Society members were allowed to do this.

My most recent visits to Goathland and Whitby were in the years 1979, 1980 and 1981. The feelings of sadness induced by the sight of the remains of the magnificent coastal line, and of Whitby locomotive shed being used as a boat-builder's workshop, were happily more than counteracted by the pleasures of the North Yorkshire Moors Railway.

Above *'A4' 'Pacific' Sir Nigel Gresley — in garter blue with red wheels — leaving York on the train we had just left on our journey to Whitby, 8 August 1949. The journey concluded behind 'Hunt' Class 4-4-0 The Craven.*

Below *Thompson Class 'A1' 'Pacific' No 60127, then in blue livery, entering York on our train for King's Cross. Note the cancelled colour light signals ready to replace the North Eastern Railway lower quadrant and LNER upper quadrant semaphore signals. 22 August 1949.*

147

Above *The classic view of Whitby locomotive shed with the abbey ruins in the background. Class 'J24' 0-6-0 No 65628 faces inside-cylinder 4-6-2T No 69794 on 10 August 1949.*

Below *Class 'J24' No 5621 at Whitby shed on the same day.*

Above *Class 'G5' tank engine No E7335 at Whitby shed, 10 August 1949.*

Below *Class 'A6' tank engine seen at the coaling stage, Whitby shed, during the same visit.*

150   **Above** *No 69794 approaching Whitby West Cliff from Sandsend with a train of ex-LMS carriages on 11 August 1949.*

Below *Class 'A8' 4-6-2T No 69858 on the 2.45 pm train from Sandsend crossing Upgang viaduct (just visible in the background of the picture above) on 16 August 1949.*

Above *Larpool viaduct, built 1882–84, photographed from the 2.54 train from Whitby West Cliff to Whitby Town on 9 August 1949.*

Below *Robin Hood's Bay seen from the 9.11 am Whitby West Cliff to Scarborough train as it climbed to Ravenscar on 13 August 1949. The train engine was 'A8' 4-6-2T No 69854.*

Above *Class 'A8' 'Pacific' No 69885 in Whitby Town*
152 *station on 11 August 1949.*

Below *Class 'G5' 0-4-4T No 7332 on the 11.40 am train on which we travelled to Goathland, standing in Whitby Town station on 15 August 1949.*

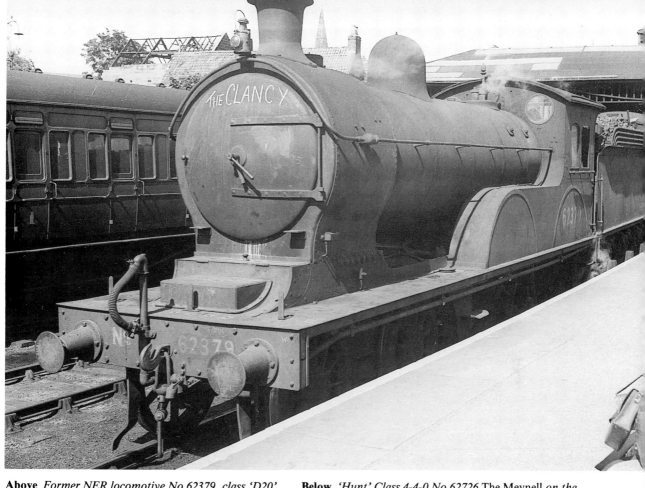

Above *Former NER locomotive No 62379, class 'D20', at Whitby Town on the 12.00 noon train to Stockton. 15 August 1949.*

Below *'Hunt' Class 4-4-0 No 62726* The Meynell *on the 9.25 am train to York in which we made the first part of our journey home on 22 August 1949.*

153

Above *'A8' 4-6-2T No 69880 takes a train north over the largest of the metal viaducts, the one at Staithes, during the afternoon of Saturday 20 August 1949.*

Below *Class 'A8' No 69882 at Whitby West Cliff station running round the train which it had brought up from Whitby Town, the 2.00 pm to Scarborough. 17 August 1949.*

Above *Class 'Q6' 0-8-0 No 63393 on a goods train bound for Whitby passing Egton station at 2.30 pm on 20 September 1962.*

Below *The same engine in the goods yard at Bog Hall, Whitby, later that afternoon.*

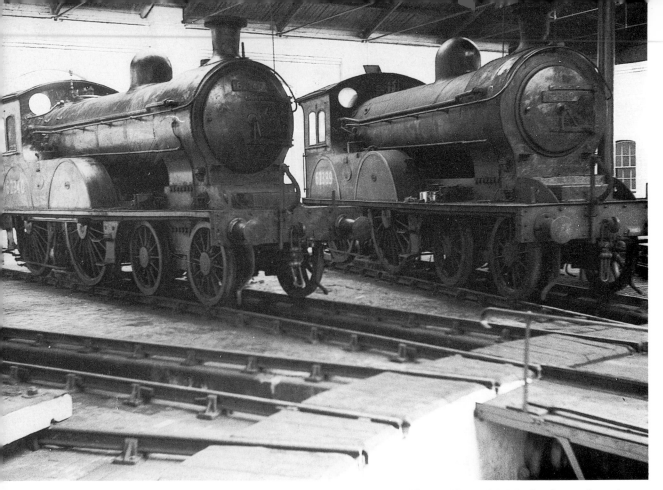

Above *Two ex-North Eastern Railway 4-4-0s, Class 'D20' Nos 62340 and 62389, in store in Scarborough shed on 12 August 1949.*

Below *Class 'A8' No 69873 in Scarborough station on the 1.03 pm train to Whitby, 12 August 1949. I had just enjoyed a ride on the footplate of this engine from the locomotive depot.*

Above *Class 'J24' 0-6-0 No 65628 passing Grosmont station on a goods train from the Esk valley line bound for Whitby on 15 August 1949. Grosmont is now at the northern end of the North Yorkshire Moors Railway.*

Below *British Railways Standard Class '3' 2-6-2T No 82029 enters Grosmont station from Pickering on the afternoon of 20 September 1962.*

157

7. HARROW

On leaving College, I started work with Kodak Ltd at the Research Laboratories in their works at Wealdstone. The northern part of the factory site adjoins the main line from Euston just beyond Harrow and Wealdstone station.

The journey by tube and train from Epsom to Wealdstone takes almost two hours, so during my 12 years in the Harrow area I lived in lodgings near to work. For 10 of those 12 years my lodgings were near to Belmont station on the Stanmore Village branch.

The Harrow & Stanmore Railway had been promoted by Frederick Gordon, a hotel entrepreneur, to serve a hotel he had established in 1885 at Bentley Priory. The railway was opened in 1890 and was worked by the LNWR. The hotel was not successful, so Gordon sold the line to the LNWR in 1899. An intermediate halt was provided at Belmont in September 1932, and this was replaced in July 1937 by the station that I knew which had an island platform and so allowed two trains to be used for peak hour services. It was pleasant living on a steam-worked branch line, and I would often use the train instead of the No 18 bus, even though the fare was more. The line was worked by engines from Watford Junction shed, usually an LMS or British Railways design 2-6-2T, but sometimes a Stanier 0-4-4T. Not surprisingly, I took photographs during the last day of passenger services beyond Belmont to Stanmore Village, 13 September 1952, and these can be seen on page 163.

Harrow and Wealdstone station was a good place for train photography in the 'fifties, and Watford Junction, with its open footbridge and locomotive shed, was better still. Fortunately, I did take pictures at each, but perhaps not as many as I would have done had I thought more of the impending electrification.

Left Fowler 2-6-2T No 40020, still bearing LMS lettering, at Harrow and Wealdstone on 13 September 1952.

Harrow, at the foot of the hill carrying the famous school, is on both the Metropolitan and the Great Central lines, and so receives trains from both Baker Street and Marylebone. When I lived in the area, the Metropolitan services to Aylesbury were hauled by electric locomotives as far as Rickmansworth, then by steam locomotives for the rest of the journey. I mostly saw Thomson Class 'L1' 2-6-4Ts, but latterly some ex-LMS 2-6-4Ts were used. A charming offshoot of the Aylesbury line was the branch from Chalfont and Latimer to Chesham (see page 167). When I travelled along this in 1951, the carriages were those which later went to the Bluebell Railway and the locomotive was an ex-Great Central Railway 4-4-2T.

During my time at Harrow, the main-line services from Marylebone to Leicester, Nottingham, Sheffield and Manchester were still running, and I saw 'Sandringham' and 'B1' Class 4-6-0s, and the occasional 'A3' 'Pacific', on these trains. The Great Central engines which I had seen at Nottingham, and also at Neasden shed, in the 'forties had all been withdrawn.

Great changes were to take place in all the railways at Harrow. In September 1960 the services from Baker Street to Amersham and Chesham were electrified and a year later those beyond Amersham to Aylesbury were

A selection of Harrow tickets.

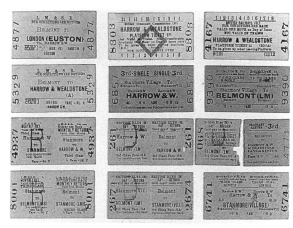

159

transferred to Marylebone. In June 1962 the quadrupling of the lines between Harrow and Rickmansworth, a major work which had been started before the Second World War, was completed. The following October saw the last of the Metropolitan compartment stock, whose inner door catches exhorted one to 'Live in Metroland'. These carriages, in their finish of varnished wood, were displaced by aluminium-clad units.

On the London Midland Region, the changes were even more far-reaching. The main line from Euston to Liverpool and Manchester was electrified with the 25kV overhead system by the end of 1965, and this was continued to Glasgow in 1974.

Fowler Class '3' 2-6-2T on a Stanmore Village train in Platform 7 of Harrow and Wealdstone station, 13 September 1952.

Above *Former LMS-design Class '2' 2-6-2T No 41220 leaves Harrow and Wealdstone on 29 October 1955.*

Below *Fowler Class '3' 2-6-2T No 40010 leaving Belmont for Harrow and Wealdstone on the morning of 12 May 1951.*

Above *Exchanging single line tokens at Belmont on 24 May 1952.*

162

Below *One of the later versions of the Ivatt 2-6-2T design, No 41320, leaving Belmont for Stanmore Village on the same day.*

Below *A wreath of flowers on the smokebox door of 2-6-2T No 40043 as it waits to take the last train from Harrow and Wealdstone to Stanmore Village on 13 December 1952.*

Above *Stanier 0-4-4T No 41909 entering Belmont from Stanmore Village on 3 September 1952.*

Below *A laurel spray on the station sign, 13 December 1952.*

Above *'Princess Royal' Class 'Pacific' No 46201* Princess Elizabeth *just north of Headstone Lane with the down 'Red Rose' express. To the right is a Bakerloo line train from Watford Junction. 16 June 1951.*

Below *Unrebuilt 'Baby Scot' No 45538* Giggleswick *on an up express passing Harrow and Wealdstone station on 29 October 1955.*

Above *Unrebuilt 'Baby Scot' No 45507* Royal Tank Corps *passing Harrow and Wealdstone on a northbound fitted freight train on 12 May 1951.*

Below *On the same day, rebuilt 'Baby Scot' No 45526* Morecambe and Heysham *passes Harrow and Wealdstone station on a down express.*

Above *Ex-LNWR Class '7F' 0-8-0 No 8896 passes Watford Junction engine shed and station on 2 October 1948.*

Below *A northbound coal train between Kenton and Harrow and Wealdstone hauled by ex-LNWR 0-8-0 No 9417 on 22 April 1951.*

Above *The Chesham branch train at Chalfont and Latimer on 16 June 1951. The engine producing the smoke was former Great Central Railway 4-4-2T Class 'C13' No 67418. The main line to Amersham and* branch line to Chesham were electrified, public services starting on 12 September 1960.
Below *Chesham station on 16 June 1951. The wooden signals are reminiscent of those used on the LB&SCR.*

8. IMPERIAL COLLEGE RAILWAY SOCIETY

I became a full-time chemistry student at Imperial College in September 1945 and it was on 20 May the following year that the first meeting of the Railway Society was held. Thus I had the pleasure of being a founder member. The meeting was a talk by O.S. Nock on 'Recent Trends in British Locomotive Design'. I will not claim to remember now the technical details of his thesis, but I do remember how, in his concluding remarks, he stressed the value of enthusiasm. It is clear from his subsequent remarkable output as a railway author that this advice was not intended only for other people.

Mr Nock had obtained his degree and Diploma of Imperial College at the City and Guilds College and this fact will, I feel sure, have influenced him in agreeing to be the Society's President from 1947 to 1950. Thus we had the pleasure of hearing him give three presidential addresses and also speak at annual dinners following addresses by other distinguished visitors: George Dow in 1947; D.S.M. Barrie in 1949; and C. Hamilton Ellis in 1950. Between 1948 and 1950, for two seasons, I was the Society's Secretary and so enjoyed correspondence with these and other notable speakers.

As well as talks, the Society arranged visits to places of railway interest, including locomotive depots, railway engineering works, signal boxes and marshalling yards. These visits provided remarkable opportunities for photography. A bellows hole spoilt the pictures I took at Neasden shed in June 1947, so my first successful photographs from a Society visit were those taken in February 1948 at the Port of London Authority locomotive shed at Woolwich. There we saw 19 locomotives: five Hudswell Clarke and six R. & W. Hawthorn 0-6-0 tanks, and eight 0-6-0 saddle tanks of the well-known design adopted by the War Department, three built by the Hunslet Engine Co and the remainder by Robert Stephenson and Hawthorn.

Most Society visits were during weekday afternoons, but two long visits, each lasting two days, were arranged during holidays. The first, on 22 and 23 April 1949, was to the Kent & East Sussex Railway, the Romney, Hythe & Dymchurch Railway and what, by the time we got there, proved to be the sad remains of the East Kent Railway. The second, on 24 and 25 March 1950, was to the Isle of Wight. Both were blessed with fine weather.

The journeys made during the first two-day visit were as follows:

Friday 22 April 1949

From	To	Depart	Arrive	Train engine
Charing Cross	Headcorn	11.15 am	12.23 pm	34079 *141 Squadron*
Headcorn	Rolvenden	12.30 pm	1.13 pm	1390 Class '01'
Rolvenden	Robertsbridge	4.40 pm	5.25 pm	32644 Class 'A1X'
Robertsbridge	Hastings	5.41 pm	6.10 pm	30922 *Marlborough*
Hastings	Ashford	6.54 pm	7.44 pm	1744 Class 'D'
Ashford	Appledore	7.52 pm	8.06 pm	31329 Class 'H'
Appledore	New Romney	8.11 pm	8.45 pm	32380 Class 'D3'

Saturday 23 April 1949

From	To	Depart	Arrive	Train engine
New Romney – Dungeness – Hythe		10.15 am	11.15 am	No 1 *Green Goddess*
Sandling Junc	Dover Priory	11.52 am	12.08 pm	1548 Class 'H'
Dover Priory	Shepherd's Well	5.15 pm	5.30 pm	1501 Class 'D'
Shepherd's Well	Faversham	7.15 pm	7.59 pm	31247 Class 'D1'
Faversham	Victoria	8.50 pm	10.21 pm	30795 *Sir Dinadan*

Left *Ex-LNWR 0-6-0ST* Earlestown *outside its shed at Wolverton Carriage Works on 9 February 1949.*

The first objective of this visit, the Kent & East Sussex Railway, had opened, as the Rother Valley Railway, from Robertsbridge — on the South Eastern's Tonbridge to Hastings line — to Tenterden on 2 April 1900. Despite its name, Tenterden station was two miles from the town. When, three years later, a station was opened which was actually convenient for the town, it was proudly named 'Tenterden Town', and the original Tenterden station became 'Rolvenden'. The line was extended a second time, to Headcorn on the Tonbridge–Ashford line, in 1905. It was then that the name of the railway was changed to the K&ESR. It should be mentioned that Col H.F. Stephens, a man who came to be associated with no fewer than 11 light railways, was General Manager and Engineer of the line for many years.

During our stop at Rolvenden, we walked to where 'Terrier' No 32678 had come off the line and were able to photograph the K&ESR's own 'Terrier', No 3, as it passed its less fortunate sister engine (see page 176). Whilst referring to the locomotive stock, I will point out that I illustrate another of the line's own engines in this collection, No 4 *Hecate*, on page 174. This Hawthorn Leslie 0-8-0T was delivered to Rolvenden in 1904 but was soon found to be over-heavy for some of the line's bridges. Ultimately, in 1932, the engine was exchanged with the Southern Railway for a Beyer Peacock 0-6-0ST dating from 1876.

The Kent & East Sussex line was closed on 4 January 1954, but a preservation society was formed and was able, after a struggle, to reopen the section from Tenterden Town to Rolvenden on 3 February 1974.

The second objective of the two-day visit was the charming, but highly professional, Romney, Hythe & Dymchurch Railway. This 15 in gauge system is still very much alive. The idea to build a 'serious' narrow gauge railway came to Captain J.E.P. Howey and his Polish friend, Count Zborowski the Younger. They were both racing motorists and, of more relevance here, steam engine addicts. The two friends made a pact to find a site for a railway as soon as possible and then proceed to make one. Tragically, Count Zborowski was killed on the Monza track at Turin, but Captain Howey kept to the pact he had made and with

the help of Sir Herbert Walker, General Manager of the Southern Railway, was directed to an ideal site, a 9-mile stretch of coast between Hythe (served by a Southern branch from Sandling Junction on the Ashford–Dover line) and Littlestone-on-Sea (served by a Southern branch from Appledore, on the Ashford–Hastings line, to a terminus called New Romney). He built his railway, and the Duke of York, later King George VI, drove the first train from New Romney to Hythe on 5 August 1926. Just under a year later, in June 1927, the line was opened to the public. In 1928 and 1929, the route was extended by 5½ miles to Dungeness lighthouse where a turning loop was provided.

Except for a pair based on Canadian Pacific designs, the Romney, Hythe & Dymchurch engines, both 4-6-2s and 4-8-2s, owe much in appearance to Sir Nigel Gresley's handsome 'Flying Scotsman' Class 'Pacifics' and 'Green Arrow' 2-6-2s.

The second two-day visit was to the Isle of Wight. Considering that this island is only 22 miles wide and 14 miles from top to bottom, it has a surprisingly complicated railway history. At the grouping in 1923, the Southern Railway took over three companies, the Isle of Wight Railway, the Isle of Wight Central Railway and the Freshwater, Yarmouth & Newport Railway, and the second of these was an amalgamation of four lines, the Cowes & Newport, Ryde & Newport, and Isle of Wight (Newport Junction) Railways, and the Newport, Godshill & St Lawrence Railway. The opening dates and lengths of the various routes were as follows (I quote the lengths of line opened by the dates shown; the start of the Ryde to Newport route traversed the northern part of the line to Ventnor, as far as Smallbrook Junction, and so the route mileage was approximately 9):

Route	Date opened	Length (miles)
Newport to Cowes	1862	4¼
Ryde to Ventnor	1866	11¼
Ryde to Newport	1875	8
Newport to Sandown	1879	9¼
Ryde (St John's Road) to Pier Head	1880	1¼

Brading to Bembridge	1882	2¾
Freshwater to Newport	1889	12
Merstone to Ventnor		
West	1900	6¾
	Total:	55½

Our planned itinerary did not include travel over the western tip of the system, the two miles from Freshwater to Yarmouth. On arrival at Yarmouth, what should we see but a bus labelled 'Freshwater'! In we got, and that is how we were able to travel over the whole system after all.

The journeys we made throughout the tour were as follows:

Friday 24 March 1950

From	To	Depart	Arrive	Train engine
Waterloo	Brockenhurst	9.30am	11.55am	34058 *Sir Frederick Pile*
Brockenhurst	Lymington Pier	12.02pm	12.15pm	30051, Class 'M7'
Lymington Pier	Yarmouth	12.40pm	1.10pm	*Farringford* ferry
Freshwater	Newport	1.55pm	2.32pm	32 *Bonchurch*
Newport	Merstone	4.08pm	4.21pm	27 *Merstone*
Merstone	Ventnor West	4.25pm	4.47pm	36 *Carisbrooke*
Ventnor West	Merstone	4.57pm	5.19pm	36 *Carisbrooke*
Merstone	Sandown	5.23pm	5.38pm	32 *Bonchurch*
Sandown	Newport	6.08pm	6.35pm	(not noted)
Newport	Cowes	6.38pm	6.50pm	(not noted)
Cowes	Ryde (Esplanade)	7.25pm	8.06pm	29 *Alverstone*

Saturday 25 March 1950

From	To	Depart	Arrive	Train engine
Ryde (Esplanade)	Ventnor	9.27am	10.12am	19 *Osborne*
Ventnor	Brading	10.42am	11.07am	19 *Osborne*
Brading	Bembridge	11.00am	11.18am	14 *Fishbourne*
Bembridge	Brading	11.32am	11.40am	14 *Fishbourne*
Brading	Ryde (St John's)	12.07pm	12.14pm	(not noted)
Ryde Pier Head	Portsmouth Harbour	2.35pm	3.05pm	Ferry
Portsmouth Harbour	Fratton	(not noted)		Electric train
Fratton	Havant	(not noted)		Electric train
Havant	Hayling Island	(not noted)		32646, Class 'AIX'
Hayling Island	Havant	(not noted)		32646, Class 'A1X'
Havant	Waterloo	(not noted)		Electric train

All our journeys on the island were made behind Class '02' 0-4-4Ts, but we did see one of the ex-LB&SCR 0-6-0Ts, No 1 *Medina*, on a goods train which we passed in Wroxall station during our journey down to Ventnor. For me the most memorable event of the tour was a footplate ride for the return from Bembridge to Brading (page 185). At Bembridge the engine had been released from its train by means of a small turntable — a rare survival of a practice quite usual in the early days of railways when all engines were small.

The journey back to London as originally planned had included an hour's stop at Guildford with a visit to the locomotive shed there. As actually carried out, it was even more interesting. We first visited Fratton shed, where one of the 'Terriers' just back from the Isle of Wight (No W13 *Carisbrooke*, in its green livery but renumbered 32677) was hiding inside, and then made a return journey on the Havant-Hayling Island branch behind another ex-Isle of Wight 'Terrier', No 32646 (page 186), formerly W8 *Freshwater*.

Above *Class 'N7' 0-6-2T No 9662 at North Woolwich on 14 February 1948, taken during the Society's journey to see the PLA railway.*

Below *The Society visited the Longmoor Military Railway on 26 April 1948. Looking splendid in royal blue livery with red lining was WD 2-8-0 No 79250 Major General McMullen.*

Above *Ex-Metropolitan Railway 4-4-4T, as LNER No 7512, Class 'H2', awaiting scrapping at Stratford on 10 March 1948.*

Below *Hill-design 0-4-0T Class 'Y4' at Stratford Works on the same day. To my mind, this was the most handsome 0-4-0T design, and I made a model of No 8127.*

Above *Hawthorn Leslie 0-8-0T No 949* Hecate, *built in 1904, which came to the Southern Railway from the Kent & East Sussex Railway and was designated class 'KES'. This engine was often to be seen shunting empty passenger stock at Clapham Junction but is seen here* acting as shed pilot at Nine Elms. Taken during the Society visit on 2 March 1949.

Below *Unrebuilt 'Royal Scot' No 46140* The King's Royal Rifle Corps *on the turntable at Camden shed during the Society visit of 8 March 1949.*

Above *Holder of the world speed record for a steam locomotive, 126 mph, No E22* Mallard *at King's Cross shed, during a visit of 16 March 1949.*

Below *Our train from Headcorn on arrival at Rolvenden, K&ESR. The engine is Class '01' 0-6-0 No 1390, and the picture was taken on 22 April 1949, the first day of the Society's two-day visit.*

Above *Stroudley 'Terrier', K&ESR No 3, originally LB&SCR No 70 Poplar and, after 1948, British Railways No 32670, passing sister engine No 32678, off the line, on the Kent & East Sussex Railway.*

176

Below *Romney, Hythe & Dymchurch 'Pacific' No 1 Green Goddess at New Romney waiting to leave on the 10.15 am train to Dungeness on Saturday 23 April 1949.*

Above *Class 'T9' 4-4-0 No 722, converted for oil burning, in the sidings at Eastleigh Works on 4 July 1949. The oil-burning project was abandoned because of the shortage of foreign currency for buying oil.*

Below *The most interesting engine we saw at Eastleigh was Adams Class 'X6' 4-4-0 No 657 in pre-war livery, which at the latest would have been withdrawn from service in 1946. The Class 'T3' 4-4-0 No 563 in the National Collection is similar in appearance but has smaller driving wheels.*

177

Above *Ex-Plymouth, Devonport & South Western Junction Railway 0-6-2T No 4 as British Railways No 30757* Earl of Mount Edgcumbe, *beautifully repainted, inside Eastleigh Works on 4 May 1949.*

Below *'M7' Class No 48 on a push-pull train at Alton after our arrival from Eastleigh, 4 May 1949. The far side of the platform at which the train is standing is now used by the Mid-Hants Railway Preservation Society, the 'Watercress Line'.*

Above *Class 'E4' 2-4-0 No 62797 at Stratford Works on 18 May 1949. The engine has a side-window cab fitted for when, as LNER No 7416, it worked on the Darlington-Penrith trains before the war.*

Below *A scene at Willesden Motive Power Depot (code 1A) during the Society visit on 25 May 1949. In the background is No 42966, one of the 40 engines which Stanier built as a taper-boilered version of the Hughes Class '5F' 2-6-0s.*

Above *Hawthorn Leslie 0-6-0T* A.S. Harris *absorbed as Plymouth, Devonport & South Western Junction Railway No 3 in 1922 by the LSWR and becoming Southern Railway No 756. The engine is seen at Stewart's Lane shed during the Society visit of 8 June 1949.*

Below *Engines outside Hither Green shed on 12 October 1949. This shed provided motive power for goods traffic from Hither Green yard via the West London Line to Willesden Junction. Class 'C' 0-6-0 goods engines, then with 108 members, the Southern Region's most numerous class, and Class 'W' 2-6-4Ts are visible.*

Above *Ex-Metropolitan Railway Class 'B' Peckett 0-6-0ST (built in 1897) as London Transport No L53 at Neasden, on 9 November 1949.*

Below *Ex-Metropolitan Railway 0-6-2Ts Nos L49 and L50 outside the locomotive shed at Neasden. Originally numbered 90 and 91 respectively, these engines were built in 1901 by the Yorkshire Engine Co (Works Nos 624 and 625) to the design of T.F. Clark.*

Above *Unreboilered 'Terrier', Class 'A1', No 680S at Lancing Carriage Works on 15 February 1950. By then the only 'Terrier' with a short smokebox, it was slightly marred by an LSWR-design chimney. The engine had originally been LB&SCR No 54* Waddon.

Below *Midland Railway Johnson-design 0-6-0T inside Kentish Town shed on 15 March 1950.*

Above *Sir Henry Fowler's version of the Johnson-Deeley Midland 'Compound', Class '4P' No 41094 at Kentish Town shed on 15 March 1950.*

Below *Coal being tipped from a wagon into the loading hopper of Kentish Town coaling plant.*

Above left *Class '02' 0-4-4T No 32* Bonchurch *waiting to leave Freshwater on the 1.55 pm train to Shanklin, by which we travelled to Newport, on 24 March 1950.*

Left *No 36* Carisbrooke *at Ventnor West on the branch train about to push its single carriage back to Merstone at 4.57 pm.*

Above *'02' No 14* Fishbourne *on the small turntable provided at Bembridge to release the engine from its train after arrival. 25 March 1950.*

Right *The view from the cab of* Fishbourne *on its return (departure 11.32 am) from Bembridge to Brading. 25 March 1950.*

Above *Engine No 19* Osborne *running round its train at Ventnor so as to be ready to take the 10.42 am train to Ryde, on which we travelled as far as Brading for our return journey on the Bembridge branch.*

Below *Just returned from the Isle of Wight, and still boasting its copper-capped chimney, 'Terrier' No 32646 (formerly LB&SCR No 46* Newington *and Isle of Wight No 8* Freshwater) *running round the Hayling Island branch train at Havant, 25 March 1950.*

Above *A moderately rare engine at Reading Signal Works, 0-6-0ST No 1925, on 3 May 1950.*

Below *Ex-London, Tilbury & Southend Railway 4-4-2T No 2097, Class '2P', at Devons Road shed, 17 May 1950.*

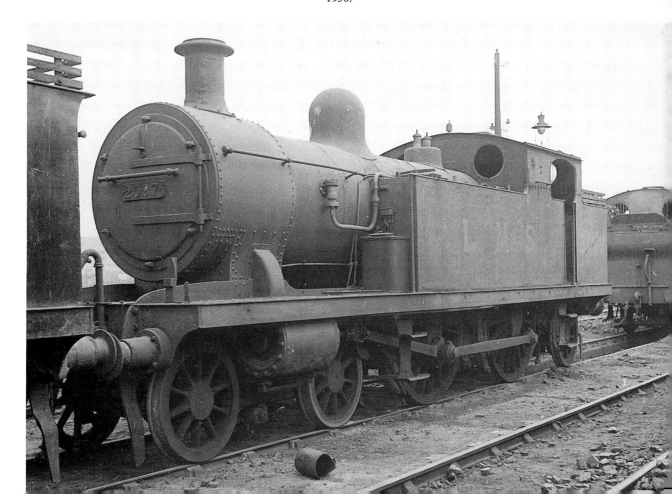

Above *Stanier three-cylinder 2-6-4T No 42518 at Devons Road shed, 17 May 1950.*

Below *Ivatt Class '4' 2-6-0 No M3004 at Wolverton station on 9 February 1949. Notice the separate plate used to prefix the number on the smokebox door.*

Above *A Corringham Light Railway train at Corringham station on 29 November 1950. This picture was taken just before work was started to reconstruct and modernize the line. The engine was one of two 0-6-0STs built by the Avonside Engineering Works, and used for passenger traffic.*

Below *An ex-War Department 2-10-0 working hard to get nowhere in the Locomotive Testing Station at Rugby on 26 October 1949.*

73788

A. N. DAVENPORT.

IMPERIAL COLLEGE

RAILWAY SOCIETY

President :

O. S. NOCK, ESQ.

SESSION

1949-1950

COMMITTEE

THE PRESIDENT

C. W. LEWIS (C. & G.), Chairman.

A. N. DAVENPORT (R.C.S.), Secretary

P. E. GALLANT (R.C.S.), Treasurer.

R. L. CHEESMAN (R.C.S.)

P. D. EVANS (C. & G.)

P. T. MOORE (R.S.M.)

G. BRIDGSTOCK (R.S.M.)

J. J. DAVIS (C. & G.)

Above *The outside of the Imperial College Railway Society programme for the 1949-50 session.* **Below** *The inside of the programme, annotated with attendances and other details by the author.*

Unless otherwise stated :

TALKS : TUESDAYS AT 5.15 p.m. IN N. 26, C. & G.

VISITS : WEDNESDAY AFTERNOONS.

—o—

WINTER TERM.

* 12th October — HITHER GREEN SHED (15)
* 18th October — M. W. EARLEY, Esq. (26)
  "The Railway Hobby"
* 26th October — RUGBY TESTING PLANT (WHOLE DAY) (15)
* 1st November — B. J. PRIGMORE, Esq. (12)
  "Modern Tramways"
* 9th November — NEASDEN (L.T.E.) SHED (9)
* 15th November — O. S. NOCK, Esq. (23)
  Presidential Address. "The Locomotive Exchanges"
* 23rd November — CLAPHAM JUNCTION SIGNAL BOX (6)
  (6 Members only).
* 29th November — J. N. MASKELYNE, Esq. (16)
  "Realism in Model Railways"
* 7th December — BRICKLAYERS ARMS SHED (8)
* 13th December — K. A. C. R. NUNN, Esq. (16)
  "Modern Railway Developments."

—o—

SPRING TERM

* 17th January — D. S. M. BARRIE, Esq. (16)
  "Progress and Problems of the British Railways"
* 18th January — CAMDEN SHED (8)

* 31st January — G. S. DEWSBERY, Esq. (17) o.s.nock present.
  "The L.D. & E.C.R."
* 1st February — BETHNAL GREEN SIGNAL BOX. (12)
* 21st (14th) February — A. DEAN, Esq. (20)
  "The Responsibilities of a Railway Civil Engineer."
* 15th February — LANCING CARRIAGE WORKS (10)
  (WHOLE DAY)
* 27th February — J. T. HOLDER, Esq. (13)
  (Monday) "The R.H. & D.R." *
* 1st March — FELTHAM SHED & YARD. (9)
  [14th March] — T. S. LASCELLES, Esq. → 2nd May. 8 for tea
  "Accidents and their influence on Signalling." (16)
* 15th March — KENTISH TOWN SHED. (8)

—o—

EASTER VACATION

22nd and 23rd April :
* TOUR OF THE ISLE OF WIGHT RAILWAYS. (8)

—o—

SUMMER TERM

* 3rd May — SIGNAL AND TELEGRAPH WORKS, READING (9)
  (WHOLE DAY.)
* 17th May — DEVONS ROAD AND PLAISTOW SHEDS.
* 18th May — DISTINGUISHED VISITOR'S ADDRESS
  AND ANNUAL DINNER. 10 for tea
  C. Hamilton Ellis, Esq.

—o—

ANY ALTERATIONS WILL BE ANNOUNCED.

BIBLIOGRAPHY

Details of locomotives:

ABC's of LMS, LNER, GWR, SR and British Railways Locomotives, various editions (Ian Allan, London)

Burtt, F. *LB&SCR Locomotives* (Ian Allan, Staines, 1946)

Burtt, F. *SE&CR Locomotives* (Ian Allan, London, 1947)

Burtt, F. *L&SWR Locomotives* (Ian Allan, London)

Casserley, H.C. *British Locomotive Names of the Twentieth Century*, Rev ed (Ian Allan, London, 1967)

Wildish, G.N. *Engines of War*, (Ian Allan, London, 1946)

Details of line closures:

Daniels, G., and Dench, L. *Passengers No More*, 3rd ed (Ian Allan, London, 1980)

Historical information:

Epsom

Dendy-Marshall, C.F., revised by Kidner, R.W. *A History of the Southern Railway*, 2nd ed, 2 vols (Ian Allan, London, 1963)

Ellis, C. Hamilton *The London, Brighton and South Coast Railway* (Ian Allan, London, 1960)

Jackson, A.A. *The Horton Light Railway* (*The Railway Magazine*, October 1981, pp 478-9)

Kirkby, J.R.W. *The Banstead and Epsom Downs Railway* (Oakwood Press, 1983)

Mitchell, V., and Smith, K. *Southern Main Lines — Epsom to Horsham* (Middleton Press, 1986)

Owen, N. *The Tattenham Corner Branch* (Oakwood Press, 1978)

Turner, J.H. *The London, Brighton and South Coast Railway*, Vol 1 Origins and Formation, Vol 2 Establishment and Growth, Vol. 3 Completion and Maturity (B.T. Batsford Ltd, London, 1977-9)

Williams, R.A. *The London & South Western Railway*, Vol 1 The Formative Years, Vol 2 Growth and Consolidation (David and Charles, Newton Abbot, 1968 and 1973)

London

Davis, H.G. *Waterloo Station Centenary, 1848-1948* (British Railways (Southern Region), 1948)

Jackson, A.A. *London's Termini* (David and Charles, Newton Abbot, 1969)

Mitchell, V., and Smith, K. *Southern Main Lines — Victoria to East Croydon* (Middleton Press, 1987)

Redhill–Reading

Dean, I., Neal A., and Smith, D. (Chalk Pits Museum) *Industrial Railways of the South East* (Middleton Press, 1984)

Kidner, R.W. *The Reading to Tonbridge Line* (Oakwood Press, 1974)

Derby

Radford, J.B. *Derby Works and Midland Locomotives* (Ian Allan, London, 1971)

Radford, J.B. *Rail Centres: Derby* (Ian Allan, London, 1986)

Rimmer, A. *The Cromford and High Peak Railway* (Oakwood Press, 1956)

Appleby

Allen, C.J. *Titled Trains of Great Britain* (Ian Allan, London, 1946)

Gammell, C.J. *LNER Branch Lines* (Oxford Pub Co)

Houghton, F.W., and Foster, W.H. *The Story of the Settle-Carlisle Line* (Norman Arch Pubs, Bradford, 1948)

Simmons, J. (ed) *Rail 150: The Stockton and Darlington Railway and What Followed* (Eyre Methuen, London, 1975)

Whitby

Hoole, K. *The Whitby, Redcar and Middlesbrough Union Railway* (Hendon Pub Co, Nelson, 1981)

Joy, D. *The Whitby and Pickering Railway* (Dalesman, 1969)

Lidster, J.R. *The Scarborough and Whitby Railway* (Hendon Pub Co, Nelson, 1977)

Harrow

Cooper, B.K. *British Rail Handbook* (Ian Allan, London, 1981)

Lee, C.E. *The Metropolitan Line* (London Transport, 1972)

Scott, P.G. *Harrow and Stanmore Railway*, 2nd ed (Hartest Prods, 1981)

Imperial College Railway Society

Densham, P. *London Transport — Its Locomotives*, 2nd ed (Author, 1947)

Freeman, J.C., and Vondrus, I.C. *Our own Light Railway* (Corringham) (Vacuum News, Vol 2, No 5 (October) 1950)

Gotheridge, I. *The Corringham Light Railway* (Oakwood Press, 1985)

Morris, O.J. *The World's Smallest Public Railway* (RH&DR) (Ian Allan, London, 1946)

Robbins, M. *The Isle of Wight Railways* (Oakwood Press, Lingfield, 1974)

Vallance, H.A. *The Kent and East Sussex Railway* (*The Railway Magazine*, February 1935, pp 105-111)

INDEX

Page numbers in **bold** refer to colour illustrations.